BARRON'S
MATHEMATICS
STUDY
DICTIONARY

Frank Tapson

Consulting Editor, U.S. edition: Robert A. Atkins

BARRON'S

First edition for the United States and its dependencies published 1998 by
Barron's Educational Series, Inc.

This Adaptation of *The Oxford Mathematics Study Dictionary* originally published
in English in 1996 is published by arrangement with Oxford University Press.

Adapted for the American market by Robert A. Atkins, Associate Professor of Mathematics,
St. John's University, Queens, New York.

All inquiries should be addressed to:
Barron's Educational Series, Inc.
250 Wireless Boulevard
Hauppauge, New York 11788

Library of Congress Catalog Card No.: 97-35216

International Standard Book No.: 0-7641-0303-2

Library of Congress Cataloging-in-Publication Data

Tapson, Frank.
    The Barron's mathematics study dictionary / Frank Tapson ;
consulting author, Robert A. Atkins.
        p.   cm.
    Adaptation of: The Oxford mathematics study dictionary.
    Includes index.
    Summary: Includes alphabetically arranged terms of the basic vocabulary
of mathematics along with definitions for each.
    ISBN 0-7641-0303-2
    1. Mathematics—Dictionaries, Juvenile.   [1. Mathematics-Dictionaries.]
I. Atkins, Robert A.   II. Tapson, Frank.   Oxford mathematics study dictionary.
III. Title.
QA5. T36   1998
510′ .3—dc21   97-35216
                                                                CIP
                                                                AC

Introduction

This dictionary is written mainly for students in the 11–16 age group, but it should also be helpful to anyone seeking a basic knowledge of the vocabulary of mathematics, and there are words from the fascinating byways of mathematics that are outside the strict limits of a school curriculum.

This is not a dictionary of etymology, grammar, or English usage. So, for instance, there is no attempt to list every possible noun, adjective, or verb, or to list all singular and plural forms—although there is a two-page spread devoted to word origins and plurals on pp.124–125. The main purpose is to provide headwords in the form in which they are most often met in mathematics.

Any dictionary must use words to explain other words. There is no escape from this, and all users are assumed to have a grasp of nonmathematical English language. The real problem, which has been acknowledged since the time of Euclid, is that of defining the most basic words, such as *point*, *line*, *surface*, and so on. These words are defined in this dictionary, but it has to be accepted that they are "intuitive ideas" or "common notions." No matter where a start is made, understanding has to break in at some point.

Cross-referencing is always a problem in a dictionary, which usually looks at words in isolation. For that reason this dictionary is divided into a number of themes, each contained on two facing pages. This format helps readers see how words relate to one another. It is much easier to read about the circle, for instance, than to look at a series of separate entries on words such as *circle*, *diameter,* and *radius*, with diagrams for some and not for others and an inconsistent set of *see alsos*. In this way each two-page opening gives the reader a good account of a particular mathematical topic. There is a Wordfinder at the front to help in finding where a particular word is to be found.

During the writing of this dictionary, I received much help and advice from the staff of Oxford University Press and the *Oxford Mathematics* Development Office in Taunton. The dictionary has benefited from that, and I must express my gratitude for their assistance.

Frank Tapson
April 1996

How to use this book

1. Look up the word in the Wordfinder at the front of the book. It looks like this and will give you the page number(s) you need in the Dictionary.

Celsius scale 106

centi- 119

same word with different uses as shown by words in brackets → centigrade *(angle)* 13

centigrade *(temperature)* 106 ← *page on which this word is to be found*

center of rotation 110

center of symmetry 102

chord 22, 39, 44

name of a section where several related words are to be found → circle 22

circumcircle *(of a polygon)* 72

circumcircle *(of a triangle)* 112

circumference 22, 88 ← *appears on two pages although the meaning is the same— entries in order of significance*

2. Look up the page number(s). All the entries are in two-page spreads organized by topic. Read the explanations, which look like this:

word being explained

using a word that is explained elsewhere, often on the same page

rhombus   A rhombus is a **quadrilateral** whose edges are all the same length; and usually no interior *(=corner)* ← *not needed for the explanation but to help with one word*
angle is a right angle. *Its diagonals bisect each other at right angles and both are also lines of symmetry.*

words in italics are not part of the explanation but give further information

Some words or phrases have the same meaning:

power ≡ **exponent**

this *is another word for* **this**, *which has already been explained, usually on the same page*

Sometimes one word can have two meanings which are slightly different, and it is shown like this:

to emphasize a particular word

circle   A circle is EITHER a closed curve . . . .

  OR the shape . . . .

  Area of circle $= \pi \times$ Radius $\times$ Radius $= \pi r^2$

a formula is printed in a different type to make it stand out

3. Look at the diagrams (if there are any).

Wordfinder

Wordfinder

Wordfinder

Wordfinder

Wordfinder

Wordfinder

The
Dictionary

abbreviation An abbreviation is a shortened form of a word or phrase, often made by using the initial letter (or letters) of the word (or words). *Some of the more common abbreviations used in mathematics are given below.*

AP arithmetic progression

APR annual percentage rate

cm centimeter(s)

cu cubic (referring to units)

dp or **d.p.** decimal place(s)

GP geometric progression

g gram(s)

gcf or **g.c.f.** greatest common factor

kg kilogram(s)

km kilometer(s)

L or **l** liter(s)

lcd or **l.c.d.** lowest (or least) common denominator

lcm or **l.c.m.** lowest (or least) common multiple

m meter(s)

mm millimeter(s)

mod modulus

QED (quod erat demonstrandum) which was to be proved

sf or **s.f.** or **sig. fig.** significant figures

SI Système International d'Unités (international system of units)

sq square (referring to units)

acronym An acronym is an **abbreviation** that is pronounceable and is usually said as a word. *An acronym is often written with capital letters, indicating that it is not a "real" word.*

PEMDAS is an **acronym** that serves as a reminder of the order in which certain operations have to be carried out when working with equations and formulas.

Parentheses Exponents Multiplication Division Addition Subtraction

SOHCAHTOA is an **acronym** that serves as a reminder of how the trigonometric ratios for a right-angled triangle are formed. The meaning of the letters is:

Sine A   = **O**pposite ÷ **H**ypotenuse
Cosine A = **A**djacent ÷ **H**ypotenuse
Tangent A = **O**pposite ÷ **A**djacent

mnemonic A mnemonic is a device which is intended to help a person's memory. *Some mnemonics are given in the remainder of these two pages.*

order of operations An aid to remembering PEMDAS is:

Please Excuse My Dear Aunt Sally.

Euler's formula A **mnemonic** to help in remembering Euler's formula for graphs giving the relationship between faces, vertices, and edges is:

say	Fred	And	Vera	Took	Eric	Too
to remember	Faces	Add	Vertices	Take	Edges	= Two

SI prefixes A **mnemonic** to help remember the order of some SI prefixes is:

say	to	give	me	kicks	my	musicians	now	play	for	ages
to remember	tera	giga	mega	kilo	milli	micro	nano	pico	femto	atto

colors of the spectrum The order of the seven colors of the spectrum (as seen in a rainbow) is given by one of the most often quoted **mnemonics**:

say	ROY G. BIV					
to remember	red	orange	yellow	green	blue	indigo	violet

trigonometric values The numerical values of the trigonometric ratios of certain angles are given by this easily remembered table:

$$\theta = 0° \quad 30° \quad 45° \quad 60° \quad 90°$$

$$\sin\theta = \frac{\sqrt{0}}{2} \quad \frac{\sqrt{1}}{2} \quad \frac{\sqrt{2}}{2} \quad \frac{\sqrt{3}}{2} \quad \frac{\sqrt{4}}{2}$$

To get the cosine values, write the second line of values in reverse order.

π The first 8 digits of π are given by the number of letters in each of the words in this question:

may	I	have	a	large	container	of	coffee ?
3.	1	4	1	5	9	2	6

$\dfrac{1}{\pi}$ The reciprocal of π to 6 decimal places is given by the number of letters in each of the words in this question:

can	I	remember	the	reciprocal ?
.3	1	8	3	10

e The first 8 digits of e are given by the number of letters in each of the words in this sentence:

to	express	e	remember	to	memorize	a	sentence
2.	7	1	8	2	8	1	8

$\sqrt{2}$ The first 4 digits of $\sqrt{2}$ are given by the number of letters in each of the words in the answer to the question:

the root of two? I	wish	I	knew
1.	4	1	4

division of fractions An aid to remembering the process for dividing one fraction by another is the rhyme:

The number you are dividing by
Turn upside down and multiply

Example: $\frac{3}{4} \div \frac{9}{16} = \frac{3}{4} \times \frac{16}{9} = \frac{4}{3} = 1\frac{1}{3}$

coordinate pairs (x,y) A phrase to help remember the order for plotting the ordered pair (x,y) is "along the passage and up the stairs," meaning "go along to x and then up to y."

accuracy The accuracy of a number is an indication of how exact it is. *Very often in numerical work, and always with measurements (unless distinct objects are counted), the answer cannot be an exact one, so it is necessary to indicate just how accurate it is.*

approximation An approximation is a stated value of a number that is close to (but not equal to) the true value of that number. *Several reasonable approximations are always possible for any number. The one most suitable for the purpose in hand must be chosen.*
Example: 3, 3.1, and 3.14 are all approximations to π (= 3.14159...)
$\approx$ is the symbol for "approximately equal to"   *Example: $\pi \approx 3.14$*

estimation An estimation is an **approximation** of a quantity which has been decided by judgment rather than by carrying out the process needed to produce a more accurate answer. *The process might be measuring, doing a sum, or anything else of that nature.*
Examples: An estimation of the number of people in a room might be 30, when actual measurement (= counting) shows it is 27.
An estimation of the value of (23.7 × 19.1) ÷ 99.6 might be 4, or 5, or 4 and a bit. Doing the arithmetic suggests that 4.54 is a good approximation.

error The error is the difference between the value of an **approximation**, or an **estimation**, and the true value. *It may or may not have a plus (+) or minus (–) sign attached indicating whether the error is too big or too small.*

absolute error The absolute error is the actual size of the **error** with NO sign.

relative error The relative error measures the size of the **error** as a fraction of the true value.
Example: $\pi \approx 3.14$ (True value is: 3.141592653 5 ...)
Absolute error is: True value – Approximate value = 0.001592653 5 ...
Relative error is: Absolute error ÷ True value
*   = 0.001592653 5 ... ÷ 3.141592653 5 ... = 0.000506957...*
Since π is itself a never-ending decimal, the dots are used to show that none of these values is an exact one. However, sufficient figures have been used to ensure that the answer is accurate enough for all practical purposes.

percentage error The percentage error is the **relative error** as a percentage.
Example: In the above example, $\pi = 3.14$ gives an error of about 0.05%.

truncate To truncate something is to cut it short.
Example: In order to work with π in a calculation we always have to truncate the true value, because it is a never-ending decimal.

truncation error A truncation error is an **error** introduced by **truncating** a number.

order of magnitude Two values are said to be of the SAME order of magnitude if their difference is small in relation to the size of the numbers being compared. *The term is used rather loosely, and generally only with large numbers. Example: 32 million and 35 million have a difference of 3 million but, since the difference is less than 10% of either of them, it could be said that they are of the same order of magnitude.*

rounding is done when a number is **truncated** so as to minimize any error. *It is carried out on the last digit of the truncated number and is decided by the first digit of those being discarded. If the first of the discarded digits is 5 or more, then the last one of the truncated digits is increased by 1; otherwise no change is made.*
Example: π (= 3.141 59...) can be truncated to 3.14 or 3.142, etc.

rounding error A rounding error is an **error** introduced by **rounding** a number.

to the nearest ... indicates that an **approximation** has been made by **rounding** as necessary, so that the given value finishes on a digit whose **place value** is stated in "..." *Usually this is done only with whole numbers, but it can be applied to decimal fractions (to the nearest tenth, etc.). Rounding must be done.*
Example: The true attendance at a football match was 24,682, but such a number might be given as 24,680 (to the nearest 10) or 24,700 (to the nearest 100) or 25,000 (to the nearest 1000).

to ... decimal places (dp) indicates that an **approximation** has been made by **truncation** to leave only the number of digits after the decimal point stated in "..." *Rounding is usually done. It is correct to use the = sign rather than ≈*
Examples: π = 3.14 (to 2 dp)
π = 3.14159 (to 5 dp)

significant figures (sf) are used to express the relative importance of the digits in a number; the most important is the first digit, starting from the left-hand end of the number, which is not zero. *Starting with the first nonzero digit, all digits are then counted as significant up to the last nonzero digit. After that, zeros may or may not be significant; it depends on the context.*
Examples:

4 significant figures	1234	78,510	16.32	0.024 71	0.005 026
3 significant figures	1230	78,500	16.3	0.024 7	0.005 03
2 significant figures	1200	79,000	16	0.025	0.005 0
1 significant figure	1000	80,000	20	0.02*	0.005

*Note that the number 0.02 has been rounded according to the evidence of the value at the top of its column and not the one immediately above it.

to ... significant figures indicates that an **approximation** has been made by **truncation** to leave only the number of significant figures stated in "..." *Rounding should be done.*
Examples: π = 3.14 (to 3 sf)   π = 3.14159 (to 6 sf)

nominal value The nominal value of a number is the "named" amount or, in the case of a measurement, the size it is intended to be.

tolerance is the amount by which a **nominal value** may vary. *Its greatest use is in the manufacturing industries.*
Example: A piston diameter is given as 65 mm ± 0.015 mm, so it has a nominal diameter of 65 mm but could be as small as 64.985 mm or as big as 65.015 mm.
The error allowed is not always evenly spread, as in $76^{+0.023}_{-0.037}$ mm.

algebra is the branch of mathematics that deals with generalized arithmetic by using letters or symbols to represent numbers. *Any statement made in algebra is true for* ALL *numbers and not just specific cases.*
Example: $9^2 - 6^2 = 81 - 36 = 45$ is true for those numbers.
But, $x^2 - y^2 = (x + y)(x - y)$ is true for all numbers.
So, $9^2 - 6^2 = (9 + 6)(9 - 6) = 45$ and can be done with ANY *numbers.*

convention for letters In **algebra** the convention is that letters for **variables** are taken from the end of the alphabet and are usually lower case (x, y, z), while those representing **constants** are taken from the beginning of the alphabet (A, B, C, a, b, c). *This convention is not followed for formulas in which the letters used are those that best serve as reminders of the quantities being handled.*

variable A variable is a symbol (usually a letter such as x, y, z) that may take any value from a given range of values. *Unless the range of possible values is stated, any real number can be used.*

real variable A real variable is a **variable** whose values must be **real numbers**.

constant A constant is a value that is unchanged whenever it is used for the particular purpose for which it was defined. *Usually it is given as a number, but in some cases a letter might be used to indicate that a constant (of the correct value) must be put in that place.*

coefficient A coefficient is a **constant** attached in front of a **variable**, or a group of variables, where it is understood that once the value of the variable(s) has been worked out, then the result is to be multiplied by the coefficient. *The absence of a coefficient is equivalent to a 1 being present.*
Example: In $3x$ $7xy$ Ax^2y y^2 the coefficients are 3, 7, A, and 1

expression An expression in **algebra** is most often a collection of quantities, made up of **constants** and **variables**, linked by signs for operations and usually not including an equals sign. *In practice it is an imprecise word and is used very loosely.*
Examples: $x + y$ $3 + x^2 - y$ $4(x - y)$ $3x^2 + 5y$ are all expressions.

literal expression A literal expression is an **expression** in which the **constants** are represented by letters as well as the variables.
Examples: $Ax^2 + Bx + C$ and $ax + b$ are literal expressions.

term The terms in a simple algebraic **expression** are the quantities that are linked to each other by means of $+$ or $-$ signs. *In more complicated expressions the word "term" is given a much looser meaning.*
Example: $5x^2 + 3x - xy + 7$ has four terms.

like terms are those **terms** that are completely identical in respect to their **variables**. *They must contain exactly the same variables, and each variable must be raised to the same power. The coefficients can be different. Like terms are identified so that they may be collected together by addition or subtraction.*
Examples: Some pairs of like terms are $3x$ and $5x$; $7x^2y$ and x^2y

constant term A constant term in an **expression** or **equation** is any **term**, or terms, consisting only of a **constant** with no **variables** attached. *Often it is merely referred to as a "constant" of the equation.*
Example: In 5x + y + 2 the coefficients are 5 and 1; the constant term is 2

equation An equation is a statement that two **expressions** (one of which may be a constant) have the same value.
Examples: 2x + 7 = 15 and 3(x + 5) = 3x + 15 are both equations.

conditional equation A conditional equation is an **equation** which is true only for a particular value, or a number of values, of the variable(s).
Example: 2x + 7 = 15 is true only when x = 4

identity An identity in **algebra** is an **equation** that is true for ALL values of the variable(s). *Strictly speaking, the ≡ sign should be used instead of the = sign, to show that it is an identity, but usually this is done only for emphasis.*
Examples: $x^2 - y^2 \equiv (x + y)(x - y)$ $3(x + 5) \equiv 3x + 15$

formula A formula is a statement, usually written as an **equation**, giving the exact relationship between certain quantities so that, when one or more values are known, the value of one particular quantity can be found.
Example: For a sphere of diameter d the volume can be found from the formula $V = \pi d^3 \div 6$

transpose To transpose an **equation** or **formula** is to rearrange it (under definite rules) to produce an equivalent version. *This is usually done in order to simplify it or make it easier to work with.*
Example: The equation 4x + y = 5 can be transposed to y = 5 – 4x

solving for a variable in a formula is **transposing** it so that the value of a different quantity from that given can be worked out.
Example: The formula $A = \pi r^2$ can be rearranged to give $r = \sqrt{\dfrac{A}{\pi}}$

simplify To simplify an algebraic **expression**, gather all **like terms** together into a single term.
Example: $2x^2 + 9 - 7x + 3xy + 5x + x^2 - 1$ simplifies to $3x^2 - 2x + 3xy + 8$

substitution A substitution in algebra is done by replacing one **expression**, or part of an expression, by something of equivalent value so that the overall truth of the original expression is unchanged.
Example: Given 4y + 3x = 22 and y = 2x, the second expression can be substituted for y in the first to give 4(2x) + 3x = 22, simplified to 11x = 22

elimination of a **variable** from an **expression** is the removal of that variable and is usually done by **substitution**.
Example: In the previous example under "substitution," the y in the first expression was eliminated by the use of y = 2x

nested multiplication is a way of rewriting an **expression** so that it is easier to work with when calculating values. *This is especially useful with a calculator where the value of the variable can be kept, and recalled from memory.*
Example: $4x^3 - 5x^2 + 7x - 8$ is easier to use as $[(4x - 5)x + 7]x - 8$

degree of a term The degree of an algebraic **term** is found by adding together ALL the powers of the **variables** in that term.
  Examples: $2x^3$ has degree 3; $4x^3y^2$ has degree 5; $3xy$ has degree 2

degree of an expression The degree of an **expression** is given by the highest value found among the degrees of all the terms in that expression.
  Example: $x^4 - 4x^3y^2 + 6y^2$ is an expression of degree 5 (the middle term).

linear equation A linear equation is an **equation** involving only an **expression**, or expressions, of **degree** 1. *Such an equation can be represented graphically by a straight line.*
  Examples: $y = 3x + 2$ $y = 4$ $x = 3y - 5$ are all linear equations.

quadratic equation A quadratic equation is an **equation** involving an **expression**, or expressions, containing a single variable, of **degree** 2.
  Examples: $x^2 + 3x - 5 = 0$ $3(x + 1)^2 = 0$ $4x^2 - 3x + 4 = 0$

satisfy When a value is substituted for a variable in an equation and leaves the truth of the equation unchanged, that value is said to satisfy the equation.
  Example: $x = 2$ satisfies the equation $3x + 7 = 13$, since $(3 \times 2) + 7 = 13$

solution The solution(s) of an **equation**, or a set of equations, is (are) the value, or values, of the variable(s) that will **satisfy** the equation(s).
  Example: $4x - 5 = 7$ has the solution $x = 3$, since $(4 \times 3) - 5 = 7$

unique solution A unique solution is the ONLY **solution**.
  Example: $2x + 5 = 13$ has the unique solution $x = 4$
  $x^2 = 9$ has the solution $x = 3$ but it is not unique, since $x = {}^-3$ is another.

trivial solution A trivial solution is one which is obvious and of little interest.
  Example: $x^n + y^n = z^n$ has a trivial solution $x = y = z = 0$. It has other, nontrivial solutions.

root A root of an **equation** is a value that will **satisfy** the equation which has been formed by putting an **expression**, containing one variable, equal to zero. *The number of roots possible is the same as the **degree** of the expression. Roots may be real or complex numbers.*
  Examples: $x^2 - 8x + 15 = 0$ has the 2 roots $x = 3$ or 5
  $x^3 - 4x^2 - x + 4 = 0$ has the 3 roots $x = {}^-1$, 1, or 4

trial and improvement is a method of looking for a **solution** in which a guessed-at value is put into a problem; the consequences are followed through, and, on the basis of any error found, a better guess value is made. *It is a very powerful method and capable of solving almost any kind of problem, provided that it is solvable. It is also known as "trial and error." Example: To find a root of $2x^3 + 4x - 5 = 0$ first try $x = 1$ in the expression. This gives a value of 1. Trying $x = 1.1$ gives a value of 2.062 so try $x = 0.9$ to get 0.058. Perhaps this is close enough to 0?*

independent equations A set of equations is independent if no single **equation** in the set can be made from some combination of the others.
  Example: $x + y = 7$; $2x - z = 6$ and $3x + y - z = 13$ are not independent, since the third can be made by adding the first two equations. Changing the third to $3x + y + z = 13$ would make an independent set.

system of equations A system of equations consists of two (or more) **equations** whose **variables** all take the same value at the same time. *Provided only that all the equations are* **independent,** *then n simultaneous equations containing n variables will have a unique solution. There are several ways of solving a system of equations, the most common being by a combination of substitution and elimination.*

indeterminate equation(s) An indeterminate equation is an **equation** (or a set of equations) for which any number of solutions can be found.
Example: x + 2y = 3 has solutions: 1,1   2,0.5   3,0   4, ⁻0.5 ...

Diophantine equations are **indeterminate equations** having only whole numbers for coefficients and having only whole numbers as acceptable solutions. *If the previous example were a Diophantine equation, it could only have solutions such as 1,1   3,0   5, ⁻1,   ...*

factors The factors of an **expression** in algebra are two, or more, other expressions which can be multiplied together to produce the original expression.
Example: (x + 1) and (x − 2) are factors of $x^2 − x − 2$, since
$$(x + 1)(x − 2) \equiv x^2 − x − 2$$

factorable A factorable **expression** is one which has at least two **factors**.
Example: $x^3 − 4x^2 + 3x − 12$ can be factored to $(x^2 + 3)(x − 4)$

expansion The expansion of an **expression** is carried out by doing as much as possible to make it into a collection of terms connected only by + and − signs. *Usually this entails doing as much multiplication as can be done, and removing all the brackets.*
Example: $(3x + 1)(x − 2) + 4(x − 5)$ expands to $3x^2 + x − 6x − 2 + 4x − 20$

multinomial A multinomial expression is one having two or more terms.

binomial A binomial expression is a **multinomial** having two terms.
Examples: 3x + 4   x − y   5 − 7y   are all binomial expressions.

trinomial A trinomial expression is a **multinomial** having three terms.
Examples: $3x^2 − 5x + 4$ x − y + 7   are trinomial expressions.

polynomial expression A polynomial expression is an **expression** made of two (or more) **terms** where each term consists of a **coefficient** and a **variable** (or variables) raised to some nonnegative power which must be a whole number. *The nonnegative power could be zero.*
Examples: $4x^3 − 5xy^2 + y^3 + 2$ is a polynomial but $x^2 + x^{−1}$ is not.

flow diagram A flow diagram is a drawing intended to make clear the order in which operations have to be done so as to produce a result. *While they can be used to explain any production process, they are most commonly used in mathematics as an aid to working out values of functions, formulas, etc.*
Example: $y = 3x^2 + 5$ is shown in this flow diagram:

Enter x → Square it → × 3 → + 5 → gives y

function machine ≡ **flow diagram**. *Usually drawn in an informal style.*

mapping A mapping is the matching of the **elements** from one **set** to the elements of another set by use of a rule. *The elements are usually numbers of some type (integer, real, complex, etc.) or they could be algebraic.*

mapping diagram A mapping diagram is a drawing used to show the effect of a **mapping** by listing the two sets and drawing arrows indicating how the elements are to be matched.
Example: The mapping diagram (right) shows what happens for the rule "multiply by 3 and add 1" for some values.

$$1 \rightarrow 4$$
$$2 \rightarrow 7$$
$$3 \rightarrow 10$$
$$4 \rightarrow 13$$

one-to-one correspondence A one-to-one correspondence occurs when a **mapping** between two sets of the SAME size pairs the elements of each set without using any element twice. *The mapping diagram above shows a one-to-one correspondence.*

domain The domain is the set that the **mapping** is coming FROM.

codomain The codomain is the set that the **mapping** is going TO.

range The range of a mapping is made up of those elements in the codomain which are actually used in the mapping.
Example: The mapping on the right uses the same set for both the domain and codomain and the rule "multiply by 2." The range is only the even numbers.

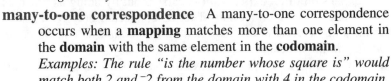

many-to-one correspondence A many-to-one correspondence occurs when a **mapping** matches more than one element in the **domain** with the same element in the **codomain**.
Examples: The rule "is the number whose square is" would match both 2 and ⁻2 from the domain with 4 in the codomain. The rule "is the child whose mother is" could match more than one child to one woman.

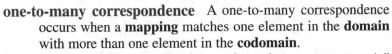

one-to-many correspondence A one-to-many correspondence occurs when a **mapping** matches one element in the **domain** with more than one element in the **codomain**.
Examples: The rule "is the number whose square root is" would match 4 from the domain with both 2 and ⁻2 from the codomain.
The rule "is the mother of" could match one woman to more than one child.

function A function is a **mapping** which involves either a **one-to-one correspondence** or a **many-to-one correspondence**. *The sets to be used for the domain and codomain must be defined; they can be the same.*
Example: For positive numbers the mapping "is the square of" is a function.

$f(x)$ is the symbol for a **function** involving a single **variable** identified in this case as *x. This is only a general statement and a definition of what $f(x)$ actually does is needed before it can be used. It is usually defined by means of an algebraic expression.*
Examples: $f(x) \equiv 3x + 1$ $f(x) \equiv 4x^2 + 3x - 7$ $f(x) \equiv 2x(x-8)$

$y = f(x)$ is a way of saying that there is a **function** of x which produces a **mapping** from x-numbers to y-numbers, though it does not say how the mapping is actually done.

Example: Given $f(x) \equiv 2x + 3$, then $y = f(x)$ is the same as $y = 2x + 3$

inverse function An inverse function is a second **function** that reverses the direction of the **mapping** produced by a first function. *For an inverse to exist, the first function must produce a one-to-one mapping. Sometimes a function can be forced into being of the one-to-one type by restricting the numbers to be used in the domain and codomain.*

Example: $f(x) \equiv x^2$ is a function of x producing a many-to-one mapping, since x or ^-x will both produce the same value of $f(x)$. This means that, though the mapping can be reversed (using square roots), it is one-to-many and therefore not a function. If the restriction is made that only positive numbers are allowed, then $f(x)$ is a one-to-one mapping and an inverse function exists.

$f^{-1}(x)$ is the symbol for the **inverse** of $f(x)$.

independent variable The independent variable in a **mapping** is the element or number FROM which the mapping STARTS. *In the mapping (right) for $f(x) \rightarrow x^2 - 1$ the values of the independent variable are $\{1, 3, 4, 5, 6, 7, 8\}$. The usual symbol is x.*

dependent variable The dependent variable in a **mapping** is the element or number TO which the mapping GOES. *In the mapping (right) for $f(x) \rightarrow x^2 - 1$, the values of the dependent variable are $\{0, 8, 15, 24, 35, 48, 63\}$. The usual symbol is y or $f(x)$.*

$$
\begin{array}{ccc}
1 & \rightarrow & 0 \\
3 & \rightarrow & 8 \\
4 & \rightarrow & 15 \\
5 & \rightarrow & 24 \\
6 & \rightarrow & 35 \\
7 & \rightarrow & 48 \\
8 & \rightarrow & 63 \\
\end{array}
$$

explicit function An explicit function is a **function** that is given entirely in terms of the **independent variable**.

Examples: $f(x) \equiv 2x + 5 \quad y = x^2 + 3 \quad f(x) \rightarrow x(x - 1) \quad$ are all explicit.

implicit function An implicit function is a **function** that is given in terms of both the **independent** and the **dependent variables**. *Implicit functions are usually written in a way that equates them to zero.*

Example: $x^2 + 2xy - y^2 = 0$

$F(x,y)$ is the symbol for an **implicit function** involving two variables, identified in this case as x and y.

bounds are two limits that values of a particular function cannot be greater or less than. The UPPER bound is a limit above which the function can produce no higher values. The LOWER bound is a limit on the lowest values. *It is usual to make the bounds as tight as possible. It may, or it may not, be possible for values to actually touch the stated bounds.*

Example: Given $f(x) \equiv 2(\sin x + 1)$, then $f(x)$ has an upper bound of 4 and a lower bound of 0, since its value cannot go above or below those limits.

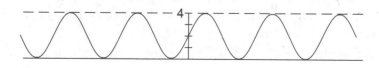

angle An angle is made when two straight lines cross or meet each other at a point, and its size is measured by the amount one line has been turned in relation to the other.

full turn A full turn is a measure of the **angle** made when the line which is turning has moved right around and returned to its starting position.

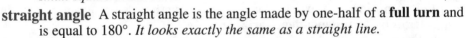

degree A degree is the angle made by $\frac{1}{360}$ th part of a **full turn**. *This means that there are 360 degrees in a full turn or, as it is usually said, "There are 360 degrees in a circle."*

minute A minute is the angle made by $\frac{1}{60}$ th part of a **degree**.

second A second is the angle made by $\frac{1}{60}$ th part of a **minute**.

There is an increasing tendency to use degrees and decimal fractions rather than minutes and seconds, except in navigation.

° ′ ″ are the symbols for degree, minute, and second respectively.
Example: 103° 26′ 47″ is 103 degrees 26 minutes 47 seconds.
In decimal form this is about 103.446°.

right angle A right angle is the angle made by one-quarter of a **full turn** or 90°. *It is usually shown on drawings by means of a small square in the corner.*

straight angle A straight angle is the angle made by one-half of a **full turn** and is equal to 180°. *It looks exactly the same as a straight line.*

acute angle An acute angle is one which is LESS than a **right angle**.

obtuse angle An obtuse angle is one which is MORE than a **right angle** but LESS than a **straight angle**.

reflex angle A reflex angle is one which is MORE than a **straight angle** but LESS than a **full turn**.

complementary angles are a pair of angles which add together to make 90°.
Example: Angles of 30° and 60° are complementary.

complement The complement of an angle is the amount needed to be added on to make 90°.   *Example: The complement of 70° is 20°.*

supplementary angles are a pair of angles which add together to make 180°.
Example: Angles of 30° and 150° are supplementary.

supplement The supplement of an angle is the amount needed to be added on to make 180°.   *Example: The supplement of 70° is 110°.*

conjugate angles are a pair of angles which add together to make 360°.

grade or **grad** A grade is the angle made by $\frac{1}{100}$ th part of a **right angle**.

centigrade A centigrade is the angle made by $\frac{1}{100}$ th part of a **grade**.
> *Grades and centigrades are now rarely used for angle measurement, though they are often found on calculators under the label* GRA.

radian A radian is the angle made at the center of a circle between two radii when the length of the arc on the circumference between them is equal to the length of one radius. *This unit of angle measurement is used a lot in further mathematical work.*

> There are 2π radians in a full turn.
> There are π radians in 180°
> To change radians into degrees, multiply by 180 and divide by π
> To change degrees into radians, multiply by π and divide by 180

positive angle A positive angle is one measured in the counterclockwise direction.

negative angle A negative angle is one measured in the clockwise direction.

> *Whether an angle is positive or negative makes no difference to its actual size, which is the same in either direction, but the distinction is sometimes needed when a movement is being explained.*

angle of elevation The angle of elevation of an object is the angle through which someone must look UP from the horizontal **plane** to see that object.
> *Example: For a person standing on level ground who sees the top of a mast at an angle of elevation of 25° the situation is represented in this diagram:*

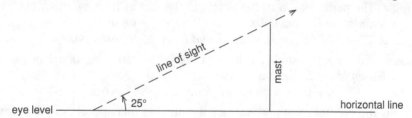

angle of depression The angle of depression of an object is the angle through which someone must look DOWN from the horizontal **plane** to see that object.
> *Example: For a person standing on a cliff looking down at a small boat and seeing it at an angle of depression of 25° the situation is represented in this diagram:*

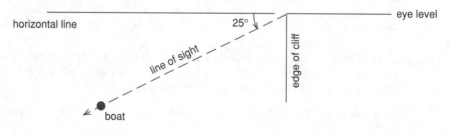

arithmetic is a part of mathematics that deals with the properties and handling of numbers, and their use in counting and calculating.

numbers are the basic elements of **arithmetic** which are used for expressing, and recording, quantities or measures of various kinds.
Examples: 2 people, 7.8 meters, the point ($^-$3, 4)

digit The digits are the single symbols 0, 1, 2, 3, 4, 5, 6, 7, 8, 9 as used in everyday **arithmetic**. *Digits are also numbers, but more importantly, they are put together to make numbers.*
Example: 2167 is a number made of four digits.

numeral ≡ **digit**.

figure A figure may be either a **digit** OR a **number**. *Both 6 and 76 are figures.*

whole number A whole number is a **number** which has no fraction attached.
Examples: 8, 13, 207 are whole numbers;   2.5 is not a whole number.

consecutive numbers are **whole numbers** that follow each other in order when arranged in a sequence from smallest to largest.
Examples: 3, 4, 5 and   19, 20, 21, 22   are both groups of consecutive numbers.

even numbers are **whole numbers** which, when divided by 2, have no remainder. *Any number which ends in 0, 2, 4, 6, or 8 must be even.*
Examples: 20, 348, 1356 are all even numbers.

odd numbers are **whole numbers** which, when divided by 2, have a remainder of 1. *Any number which ends in 1, 3, 5, 7 or 9 must be odd.*
Examples: 17, 243, 8645 are all odd numbers.

parity The parity of a **number** refers to the fact of it being either **even** or **odd**.
Examples: The numbers 4 and 10 have the same parity (both even); so do 3, 7, and 15 (all odd), while 5 and 8 are of opposite parity.

square To square a number is to multiply it by itself. *The square of 1 is 1.*
Examples: To square 6 work out 6 × 6 = 36
To square 2.5 work out 2.5 × 2.5 = 6.25

x^2 ^{2} is the symbol meaning "**square** the number that appears in the place of x"
Example: When x = 1.3, then x^2 means 1.3 × 1.3 = 1.69

square root A square root of a number is another number which when **squared** will equal the first number. *The square roots of 1 are 1 and $^-$1.*
Example: One square root of 16 is 4 since 4 × 4 = 16; another is $^-$4

$\sqrt{}$ is the symbol meaning "the **square root** of the number given."

Examples: $\sqrt{49}$ = 7 (7×7= 49) $\sqrt{3.24}$ = 1.8 (1.8 × 1.8 = 3.24)

radical A radical is the square root of a number. *It can also be a cube (or other) root and is sometimes applied to an expression which contains radicals. The square root of any prime number is irrational.*

Examples: $\sqrt{2}$ (≈ 1.414...) $2\sqrt{3}$ $\sqrt[3]{19}$ are all radicals.

perfect square A perfect square is a number whose **square root** is a **whole number**. *Examples: 1, 4, 9, 16, 25, 36, and 289 are all perfect squares (with square roots of 1, 2, 3, 4, 5, 6, and 17 respectively).*

cube To cube a number is to multiply it by itself and then multiply the result of that by the original number. *The cube of 1 is 1.*
Examples: *To cube 4 work out $4 \times 4 \times 4 = 64$*
To cube -4 work out $-4 \times -4 \times -4 = -64$

x^3 ^{3} is the symbol meaning "**cube** the number that appears in the place of x."
Example: When $x = 1.7$, then x^3 means $1.7 \times 1.7 \times 1.7 = 4.913$

cube root The cube root of a number is another number which, when **cubed**, will equal the first number. *The cube root of 1 is 1.*
Example: The cube root of 8 is 2, since $2 \times 2 \times 2 = 8$

$\sqrt[3]{}$ is the symbol meaning "find the **cube root** of the number given."

Example: $\sqrt[3]{4.096} = 1.6$, since $1.6 \times 1.6 \times 1.6 = 4.096$

digit sum The digit sum of a number is found by adding all its **digits** together.
Example: The digit sum of 742 is $7 + 4 + 2 = 13$

digital root The digital root of a number is made by finding its **digit sum** to make a new number and repeating this process on each new number made until only a single digit remains—this is the digital root of the original number.
Example: $8579 \rightarrow 8 + 5 + 7 + 9 = 29 \rightarrow 2 + 9 = 11 \rightarrow 1 + 1 = 2$,
so 2 is the digital root of 8579

casting out 9's is a method of checking on the accuracy of some arithmetic processes. *For the process of addition, subtraction, or multiplication of numbers, if the same process is applied to the digital roots of those numbers, then the digital root of that answer should be the same as the digital root of the actual answer obtained from the full numbers. If there is an error, this method will not identify where it is, only that there is one. Examples: In these sums (x) is the digital root of the preceding number.*

$$806_{(5)} + 57_{(3)} = 863_{(8)} \qquad [5 + 3 = 8] \checkmark$$
$$806_{(5)} - 57_{(3)} = 749_{(2)} \qquad [5 - 3 = 2] \checkmark$$
$$806_{(5)} \times 57_{(3)} = 45{,}942_{(6)} \qquad [5 \times 3 = 15 \rightarrow 1 + 5 = 6] \checkmark$$

order of operations From the expression $2 + 4 \times 3 - 1$ it is possible to get different answers according to the order in which the operations are done. Working from left to right ($+ \times -$) gives 17; using ($+ - \times$) gives 12; using ($\times + -$) gives 13; and using ($- \times +$) gives 10.   To prevent this from happening, there is an established order in which operations MUST be done. Anything in parentheses has to be done first, then exponents, then multiplication and division, and then addition and subtraction. An aid to remembering this is **PEMDAS**.

Examples: $(2 + 4) \times 3 - 1 = 17$ $\qquad$ $(2 + 4) \times (3 - 1) = 12$
$2 + 4 \times (3 - 1) = 10$ $\qquad$ $2 + 4 \times 3 - 1 = 13$
Even when not strictly necessary, parentheses can be helpful.

percent A value given in percent means that the number stated is to be used to make a fraction with that number on the top and 100 on the bottom.
Example: 45 percent is the fraction $\frac{45}{100}$

% is the symbol for percent. *Example: 37% is 37 percent or $\frac{37}{100}$*

per mil A value given per mil means that the number stated is to be used to make a fraction with that number on the top and 1000 on the bottom.
Example: 68 per mil is the fraction $\frac{68}{1000}$

‰ is the symbol for per mil. *Example: 21‰ is 21 per mil or $\frac{21}{1000}$*

percentage point A percentage point is the actual value of the difference between two percentages, and NOT the percentage change.
Example: A report that "a bank reduced its interest rate of 5% by 1 percentage point" means that the new rate is 5% reduced by 1 to make 4%, and not 5% reduced by 1% (of 5%) to make it 4.95%

principal The principal is the amount of money involved (usually at the start) in some transaction such as lending, borrowing, or saving.
Example: On opening an account with $250 there is a principal of $250

interest The interest is the amount of extra money paid in return for having the use of someone else's money.

rate of interest The rate of interest states how the **interest** is to be worked out.
It is usually stated as a percentage of the principal for each given period. Example: The interest on the loan is set at 2% per month.

simple interest The calculation of simple interest at the end of each **period** is always worked out only on the **principal** of the original amount. *This method is rarely used nowadays.*
Example: A loan of $300 at 2% per month at simple interest would mean that at the end of each month interest of $6 would be owing. So, at the end of a year, the total interest owing would be $72 (plus the loan still has to be repaid).

$$\text{Total simple interest} = \frac{\text{Principal} \times \text{Rate of interest (\%)} \times \text{Number of periods}}{100}$$

compound interest The calculation of compound interest at the end of each **period** is worked out on the **principal** plus ANY PREVIOUS INTEREST already earned. *This is the usual method nowadays. In this case, it is the total amount owing that is calculated, rather than the separate interest.*

$$\text{Total amount owing} = \text{Principal} \left(1 + \frac{\text{Rate of interest (\%)}}{100} \right)^{\text{Number of periods}}$$

depreciation The depreciation of the value of an object is the amount by which that value has fallen. *It is similar to compound interest, except that the value is decreasing. If the rate of depreciation (as a % per period) is known, then the new value can be worked out from this formula:*

$$\text{New value} = \text{Original value} \left(1 - \frac{\text{Rate of depreciation (\%)}}{100} \right)^{\text{Number of periods}}$$

reverse percentage A reverse percentage is needed to find the original value of something when all that is known is its current value and the percentage (of the original value) by which its original value was INCREASED. *This is a common problem when a price including a tax is known and the price without the tax is needed.*

> Original value = (100 × Current value) ÷ (100 + R)
> where R is the percentage change made to the original value.
> The second bracket is (100 − R) if a DECREASE has been made.

Example: A lawnmower costs $540, which includes sales tax at 8%. Its cost without sales tax must be 100 × 540 ÷ (100 + 8) = $500

installment An installment is an amount of money paid at regular intervals over some agreed period of time. *Installments commonly arise in connection with repaying a loan (plus interest) or keeping up a time payment agreement. It is usual to arrange installments of equal size (payable weekly or monthly) so that the loan and the interest are paid off together. The size of installment needed to do this can be calculated from this formula:*

$$\text{Installment} = \frac{A\,R\,F^n}{(F^n - 1)} \text{ where}$$

A is amount of loan
R is rate of interest (%) per period in decimal form
$F = R + 1$
n is number of periods

Example: $300 loaned for 12 months at 2% per month compound interest.
$$A = 300, \quad R = 0.02, \quad F = 1.02, \quad n = 12$$
Monthly installments = $28.37 (to the nearest cent)

APR The APR is the **A**nnual **P**ercentage **R**ate of a loan. *Organizations that lend money express their offers in various ways in order to make them look different and attractive. The law requires that the APR also be given so that comparisons can be made more easily. There are formulas for this.*

discount A discount is an amount which is taken OFF the price of something. *Discounts are usually stated as percentages.*
Example: A price of $12 has a discount of 10%, so $1.20 is taken off.

gross A gross amount (of weight or money) is that total which exists at the beginning BEFORE any deductions are made for any reason.
Example: A person's wages are $270 (gross) but various taxes totaling $75 are taken off, so $195 is left. (This is the net wage.)

net A net amount (of weight or money) is the amount remaining AFTER any necessary deductions have been made.
Example: A packet containing rice weighs 760 grams (gross) but the packet weighs 40 grams, so the net weight of the contents is 720 grams.

rate of exchange The rate of exchange between two systems is a statement of how a value in one system may be given as an equivalent value in the other system. *It is most often used in changing money between countries.*
Example: The rate of exchange between French (francs) and British (pounds) currency might be given as 8.26 francs to the pound.

arithmetic (the four rules)

the four rules of arithmetic are the operations of **addition**, **subtraction**, **multiplication**, and **division**.

addition is the operation of combining numbers, each of which represents a separate measure of quantity, so as to produce a number representing the measure of all those quantities together. *If the number is to have any physical meaning, then the quantities must be of the same type.*
Example: Addition shows that 9 people joined by 4 people makes 13 people.

total A total is the final number produced by the process of **addition**.
Example: In 9 + 4 = 13 the number 13 is the total.

aggregate ≡ **total**

sum may mean: the process of **addition** on some specified numbers
OR: the result produced by a process of **addition** (= **total**).
Examples: "Find the sum of all the numbers from 1 to 9." "The sum of 8 and 4 is 12."

subtraction is the operation of finding a number which gives a measure of the difference in size between two quantities or measures.
Examples: Taking 9 people from a group of 13 leaves 4   (13 – 9 = 4)
$$5°C - (^-3°C) = 8°C$$

difference The difference between two numbers is the result of a **subtraction**.

absolute value The absolute value of a number is a measure of its distance from zero on the **number line**. Therefore, it is either a positive number or zero. The symbol for absolute value is $|\;|$.
Examples: $|5| = 5$ $|-5| = 5$ $|0| = 0$

decomposition is a method of **subtraction** which breaks down (decomposes) the first number in the operation, where necessary, to allow the subtraction to take place. *It works like this:*

$$\begin{array}{r} 874 \\ -629 \\ \hline \end{array} \quad is \quad \begin{array}{r} 800 + 70 + 4 \\ 600 + 20 + 9 \\ \hline \end{array} \quad which\ becomes \quad \begin{array}{r} 800 + 60 + 14 \\ -\ 600 + 20 + 9 \\ \hline 200 + 40 + 5 \end{array} \quad written\ as \quad \begin{array}{r} 8\ ^6\not7\ ^14 \\ -6\ 2\ 9 \\ \hline 2\ 4\ 5 \end{array}$$

equal addition is a method of **subtraction** which adds the same amount to both numbers, where necessary, to allow the subtraction to take place. *This is the method where the phrase "borrow and pay back" occurs. It works like this:*

$$\begin{array}{r} 874 \\ -629 \\ \hline \end{array} \quad is \quad \begin{array}{r} 800 + 70 + 4 \\ 600 + 20 + 9 \\ \hline \end{array} \quad \begin{array}{c} add\ 10\ to \\ both\ numbers \end{array} \quad \begin{array}{r} 800 + 70 + 14 \\ -\ 600 + 30 + 9 \\ \hline 200 + 40 + 5 \end{array} \quad written\ as \quad \begin{array}{r} 8\ 7\ ^1\not4 \\ -6\ ^3\not2\ 9 \\ \hline 2\ 4\ 5 \end{array}$$

counting on is a method of **subtraction** which finds the **difference** between two numbers by counting on from the smaller to the larger and then adding up all the "steps" needed. *The steps can be of any convenient size that can be handled mentally. It is sometimes called the "shopkeeper's method," from the way change used to be given.*

Example: $629 \xrightarrow{+1} 630 \xrightarrow{+70} 700 \xrightarrow{+100} 800 \xrightarrow{+74} 874 \quad =245$

complementary addition is a method of **subtraction** that makes a new number from the second number of the operation by: subtracting all its digits from 9; adding this new number to the first number of the operation; adding 1 to the answer; finally subtracting 1 from the "extra digits." *Extra digits are all those which go beyond the length of the second number.*

874	874	*adding 1 to the answer makes* **1245**
− 629 *change to*	+ 370	*only "extra digit" is left-hand 1 (take off 1 = 0)*
	1244	*and final answer =* **245**

35,874 − 629 would first give 36,244 and the extra digits would be 36. Subtracting 1 gives the final answer: 35,245

multiplication is the operation which combines several equal measures of size, giving the result as a single number. *With whole numbers, multiplication can be seen as equivalent to the addition of several numbers of the same size; the more general case for all numbers is an extension of that. Example: There are 4 rooms with 6 people in each, so in total there are 6+6+6+6 or 6 × 4 people. This extends to cases like 3.28 × 5.74*

$\times$ $*$ are two symbols, both meaning that multiplication is to be done.

product The product is the result given by the operation of **multiplication**. *Example: The product of 1.6 and 7 is 1.6 × 7, which is 11.2*

division is the operation between two numbers which measures how many times bigger one number is than the other. *With whole numbers, division can be seen as equivalent to the sharing out of a quantity into a number of equal-sized portions; the general case for all numbers is an extension of that.*

$\div$ $/$ are two symbols, both meaning that **division** is to be done. *Examples: 18 ÷ 6 = 3 and 18/6 = 3*

short division is the description used when **division** is done mentally. *Numbers may be written down, but none of the processes are.*

long division is an **algorithm** to deal with **division** for those cases where the numbers are too difficult to work with mentally. *An example is shown on the right.*

$$\begin{array}{r} 67 \\ 23\overline{)1541} \\ 138 \\ \underline{161} \\ 161 \end{array}$$

quotient The quotient is the result given by the operation of **division**. *Example: In 32 ÷ 8 = 4 the quotient is 4*

dividend The dividend is the amount in a **division** operation which is to be shared out, or the number which must be divided into parts. *Example: In 21 ÷ 3 = 7 the dividend is 21*

divisor The divisor is the amount in a **division** operation which must do the dividing, or among which the **dividend** must be shared. *Example: In 18 ÷ 9 = 2 the divisor is 9*

remainder The remainder is the amount left over in a **division** operation when one quantity cannot be divided exactly by another. *Example: In 23 ÷ 4 the answer (quotient) is 5 with a remainder of 3, which is usually written as 5 r 3 or 5 rem 3*

Dividend ÷ Divisor = Quotient *and* Remainder *that cannot be shared out*

calculus is the branch of mathematics that uses the concept of a **limit** to arrive at results. Its two main parts are **differential calculus** and **integral calculus**. *The techniques of calculus enable one to solve problems from business, science, and technology, and also from pure mathematics.*

differential calculus involves finding the rate at which a **variable** quantity is changing.

Example: When a stone is dropped from a height, its velocity and distance from the starting point vary with time. Finding its velocity and distance traveled at any instant is a type of problem solved by differential calculus.

slope of a curve The **slope** of a **line** is a number that describes the rate at which the line is rising or falling. A **curve** can also rise or fall, but the rate will be different at different points on the curve. The slope of a curve at a **point** is defined to be the slope of the **tangent** line to the curve at that point. *The slope is usually called the* DERIVATIVE *of the function. Symbols for derivative include* $\frac{dy}{dx}, f'(x),$ *and* $D_x y$.

integral calculus can be thought of as an opposite process to **differential calculus**. That is, if the rate of change of a **function** is known, the process of INTEGRATION enables one to determine the nature of the original function. *The symbol for the integral of a function is* $\int f(x)dx$.

definite integral When **limits** of integration are specified, such as in the expression $_a\int^b f(x)dx$, *the integral is known as a definite integral.*

indefinite integral When the **limits** of integration are not specified, such as in $\int f(x)dx$, *the integral is called an indefinite integral.*

maxima and minima An important application of the derivative is to find the relative maximum or minimum of a **function**. *The diagram at the right shows a relative maximum point at A and a relative minimum point at B. Note that the tangent line in each case is horizontal; that is, the slope of the tangent (the derivative) is zero. By setting the expression for the derivative equal to zero and solving the resulting equation, these maximum and/or minimum points can be determined.*

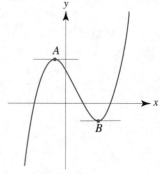

limit The concept of limit is important in the study of calculus. In calculus, the derivative is found by finding the slope of the **secant** to a curve and then allowing the distance between the points to approach, but never quite reach, zero.

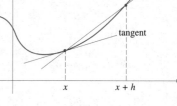

Example: In the fraction $\frac{1}{n}$, *as n becomes larger and the fraction would get closer and closer to, but never quite reach, zero. The symbol for limit is* $\lim_{x \to a} f(x)$, *which is read as "the limit of f(x) as x approaches a."*

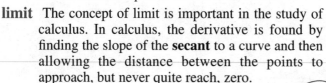

continuity A **function** is continuous in an interval if it does not have any breaks, jumps, or holes in the given interval.

Examples:

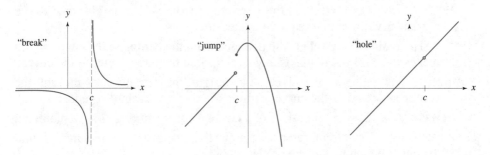

All these graphs are discontinuous at *x* = *c*.

area under a curve can be found by integration, provided the integral of the **function** generating the curve can be integrated. If the equation of the curve in the illustration is **y = f(x)**, then the shaded area is given by the definite integral $_a\!\int^b f(x)dx$, where *a* and *b* are known as the lower and upper **limits** of integration. The actual numerical value for the area is found by substituting *b*, then *a*, in the integrated expression, and subtracting.
Example: If $_a\!\int^b f(x)dx = F(x)$, the area will be F(b) – F(a). If the equation of the curve cannot be integrated, then one of the methods described on page 105 can be used.

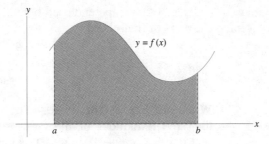

circle A circle is EITHER a **closed curve** (= *a line which curves around and joins up with itself*) in a **plane** (= *a flat surface*), which is everywhere the same distance from a single fixed point, OR it is the shape enclosed by that curve.

$$\text{Area of circle} = \pi \times \text{Radius} \times \text{Radius} = \pi r^2$$

center The center of a **circle** is the fixed point from which the distance to the closed curve forming the circle is measured.

radius The radius of a **circle** is the distance from the **center** to the curve which makes the circle. A radius is any straight line from the center to the curve.

diameter The diameter of a **circle** is a straight line which passes through the **center** and touches the curve forming the circle at each of its ends.

semicircle A semicircle is one-half of a **circle** made by cutting along a diameter.

circumference The circumference of a **circle** is the distance measured around the curve which makes the circle.

$$\text{Circumference} = \pi \times \text{Diameter} = \pi d$$

chord A chord of a **circle** is any straight line drawn across a circle, beginning and ending on the curve making the circle. *A chord which passes through the center is also a diameter. A line extending beyond the circle is a secant.*

arc An arc of a **circle** is any piece of the curve which makes the circle.

$$\text{Length of arc} = \frac{\text{Central angle of arc}}{360} \times \text{Circumference of full circle}$$

sector A sector of a **circle** is the shape enclosed between an **arc** and the two radii at either end of that arc.

$$\text{Area of sector} = \frac{\text{Central angle of sector}}{360} \times \text{Area of full circle}$$

segment A segment of a **circle** is the shape enclosed between a **chord** and one of the **arcs** joining the ends of that chord.

$$\text{Area of segment} = \left(\frac{\pi\theta}{360} - \frac{1}{2}\sin\theta \right) \times r^2 \quad \text{where}$$

θ is the angle of the segment at the center
r is the radius of the circle

major ⎫ ⎧ **arc**
      ⎬ ⎨ **sector**
minor ⎭ ⎩ **segment**

When one **arc**, **sector**, or **segment** is made in a circle, then the remainder of the circle makes another arc, sector, or segment. The LARGER is known as the MAJOR, the SMALLER as the MINOR arc, sector, or segment.

concentric circles are two or more circles which have been drawn using the SAME position for their centers.

eccentric circles are two or more circles which have been drawn using DIFFERENT positions for their centers. *Usually, for two circles, one is completely inside the other, or else there is some area which is common to all the circles.*

annulus An annulus is a ring-like shape which is formed by the space enclosed between two **concentric circles**.

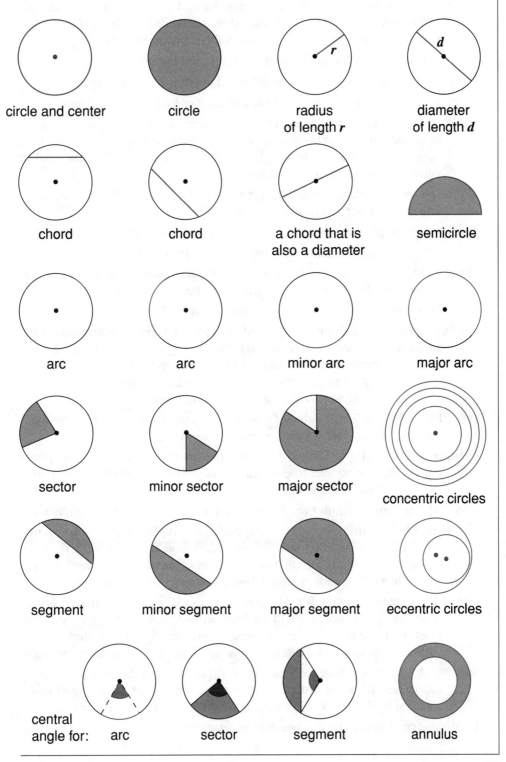

circle and center

circle

radius
of length r

diameter
of length d

chord

chord

a chord that is
also a diameter

semicircle

arc

arc

minor arc

major arc

sector

minor sector

major sector

concentric circles

segment

minor segment

major segment

eccentric circles

central
angle for: arc

sector

segment

annulus

cones, cylinders, and spheres

cone A cone is the three-dimensional shape formed by a straight line when one end is moved around a **simple closed curve**, while the other end of the line is kept fixed at a point which is not in the plane of the curve.

vertex The vertex of a **cone** is the fixed point used in making it.

base The base of a **cone** is the simple closed curve used in making it.

circular cone A circular cone is a **cone** made using a circle as its **base**.

right circular cone A right circular cone is a **cone** made using a circle as its **base** and with its **vertex** placed on a line passing through the center of the base and perpendicular to the plane of the base. *It is what is usually meant when only the word "cone" is used.*

oblique circular cone An oblique circular cone is a NON-**right circular cone**. *The vertex is not placed over the center of the base.*

height The height of a **cone** is the distance of its **vertex** above the plane of its **base**.

Volume of any cone = Area of base × Height ÷ 3

slant height The slant height of a **right circular cone** is the length of any straight line from the circumference of its **base** to the **vertex**.

Slant height = $\sqrt{r^2 + h^2}$ *r* is radius of base   *h* is height

curved surface of a cone The curved surface of a **right circular cone** is the sector which could be bent around (until the edges meet) to form the cone.

Radius of circle to make sector = Slant height of cone
Angle of sector = 360 × Base radius ÷ Slant height of cone
Area of sector = π × Base radius × Slant height of cone

frustum of a cone The frustum of a **cone** is the part of the cone cut off between the **base** and a plane which is parallel to the base.

cylinder A cylinder is formed by using two identical **simple closed plane curves** that are parallel to each other and joining up corresponding points on each of the curves with straight lines.

ends The ends of a **cylinder** are the two simple closed curves used to make it.

right circular cylinder A right circular cylinder is a **cylinder** in which the **ends** are circles and the line joining their centers is an axis of symmetry of the cylinder. *It is what is usually meant when only the word "cylinder" is used.*
Volume of a right circular cylinder = Area of one end × Distance between ends

curved surface of a cylinder The curved surface of a **right circular cylinder** is the rectangle which could be bent around (until two opposite edges meet) to fit the two circular ends and so form the complete cylinder.
Area of curved surface = $2\pi rh$ *r* is radius of end   *h* is height (or length)

sphere A sphere is EITHER the shape of a surface in three dimensions which is everywhere the same distance from a single fixed point, OR the solid shape enclosed by that surface. *The balls used to play most games are spheres.*

hemisphere A hemisphere is one-half of a **sphere**.

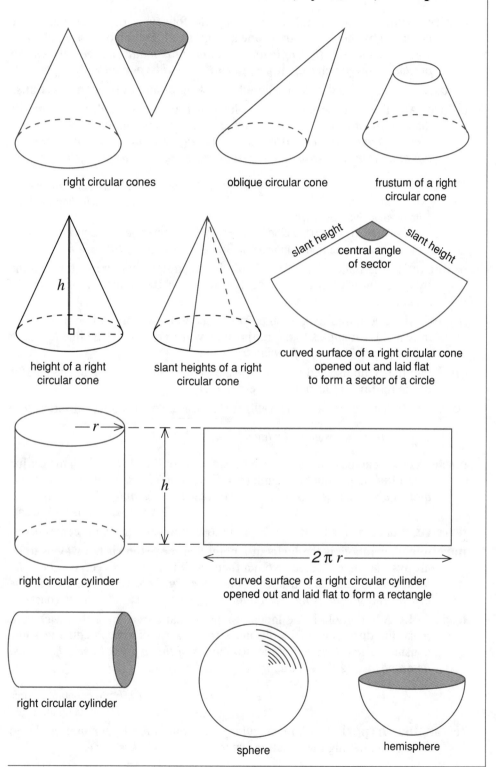

right circular cones

oblique circular cone

frustum of a right circular cone

h

height of a right circular cone

slant heights of a right circular cone

slant height

central angle of sector

slant height

curved surface of a right circular cone opened out and laid flat to form a sector of a circle

r

h

$2\pi r$

right circular cylinder

curved surface of a right circular cylinder opened out and laid flat to form a rectangle

right circular cylinder

sphere

hemisphere

conic sections is the general name given to the four types of curves that can be produced by the section of a **cone** as it is sliced through by a straight cut at various angles. *As the angle at which the cut is made changes, the curves produced are the* **circle, ellipse, parabola,** *and* **hyperbola.**

focus A focus is a fixed point used in the drawing of any of the **conic sections.**

ellipse An ellipse is the **locus** of a point which moves in such a way that its distances from two **foci** add together to a constant amount. *Once the two foci are fixed and the constant amount is decided, then only* ONE *ellipse is possible. It may be drawn as a graph using the equation*

$$\frac{x^2}{a^2} + \frac{y^2}{b^2} = 1 \quad \text{where } a, b \text{ are constant values affecting the size}$$

Its area is given by πab
Its perimeter is difficult to calculate exactly, but Ramanujan's formula gives the most accurate approximation: $\pi[3(a + b) - \sqrt{(a + 3b)(3a + b)}]$

major axis The major axis of an **ellipse** is the straight line drawn through the two foci with each end of the line touching the ellipse. *It is a line of symmetry.*

minor axis The minor axis of an **ellipse** is the longest straight line that can be drawn at right angles to the **major axis** with each end of the line touching the ellipse. *It is a line of symmetry.*

a, b are the symbols used to give the size of an ellipse, being half the lengths of the **major** and **minor** axes respectively.

eccentricity The eccentricity of an **ellipse** is a measure of how much it varies from a circle. *Its value is given by the formula* $\sqrt{1 - \frac{b^2}{a^2}}$ $\quad (a > b)$

circle A circle can be considered as a special case of the **ellipse**, with the **major** and **minor** axes equal in length $(a = b)$. *It is an ellipse with only one focus and its eccentricity is zero. It may be drawn as a graph using the equation* $x^2 + y^2 = a^2$ *(a* is the radius)

directrix A directrix is a fixed straight line used in drawing some of the conic curves.

parabola A parabola is the **locus** of a point that moves in such a way as to be always the same distance from a **focus** as it is from a **directrix.** *Once the focus and the directrix are fixed, only one parabola is possible. It may be drawn as a graph using the equation* $y^2 = 4ax$ *(a* is a constant)

hyperbola A hyperbola is the **locus** of a point that moves in such a way as to make the difference of its distances from two **foci** always equal to some constant. *The difference of the two curves of the hyperbola may be drawn as graphs using the equation*

$$\frac{x^2}{a^2} - \frac{y^2}{b^2} = 1 \quad \text{(a, b are constant values affecting the size)}$$

rectangular hyperbola A rectangular hyperbola is the **hyperbola** produced by a graph having the equation $xy = k$ *(k* is a constant)

Slicing through a cone in these directions:

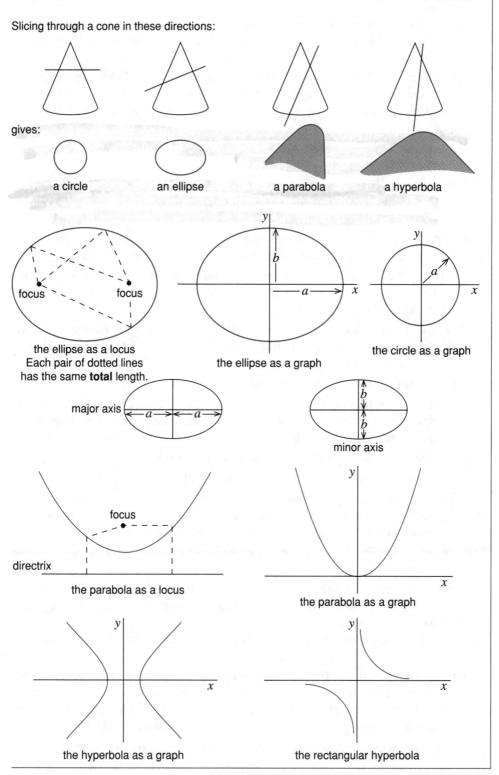

gives:

a circle   an ellipse   a parabola   a hyperbola

the ellipse as a locus
Each pair of dotted lines
has the same **total** length.

the ellipse as a graph

the circle as a graph

major axis

minor axis

the parabola as a locus

the parabola as a graph

the hyperbola as a graph

the rectangular hyperbola

27

coordinate systems are used to give the position of a point by placing it in relation to some other fixed positions. *The fixed positions might be points, lines, or planes, depending on the system.*

Cartesian coordinates give the position of a point in two-dimensional space by stating its shortest distances from two fixed reference lines set at right angles to each other. *The distances may be given as positive or negative values.*

axes The axes are the two fixed lines in the **Cartesian coordinate** system. *They are usually identified separately as the x-axis and the y-axis and are placed at right angles to each other.*

ordered pair An ordered pair is the two numbers, written in a particular order, needed to give the position of a point in the **Cartesian coordinate** system. *The convention is to give the x-number first, and the y-number second.*

origin The origin in the **Cartesian coordinate** system is the point where the two **axes** cross. *It is the point identified by the ordered pair (0,0).*

ordinate The ordinate of a point in **Cartesian coordinates** is its distance from the x-axis, as measured on the y-axis. *It is the value of the second number in the ordered pair for that point.*

abscissa The abscissa of a point in **Cartesian coordinates** is its distance from the y-axis, as measured on the x-axis. *It is the value of the first number in the ordered pair for that point.*

rectangular coordinates ≡ **Cartesian coordinates**

three-dimensional coordinates give the position of a point in three-dimensional space by using three fixed reference lines. *The third axis, identified as the z-axis, is at right angles to both the x- and y- axes. For this, an ordered triple is used.*

pole A pole is a fixed point used in **polar coordinates**.

polar axis A polar axis is a fixed line, one end of which is a **pole**.

polar coordinates give the position of a point in two-dimensional space by stating its DISTANCE from a **pole** and the size of the ANGLE between the **polar axis** and a line drawn from the point to the pole.

radius vector The radius vector is the line joining the **pole** and the point whose position is being given.

r, θ are the symbols for showing **polar coordinates**, where r is the length of the **radius vector** and θ is the angle (in radians or degrees) between the **polar axis** and the radius vector.

To change polar coordinates (r, θ) into Cartesian coordinates (x, y) use:
$$x = r \cos \theta \qquad\qquad y = r \sin \theta$$

world coordinate system Positions on the face of the earth are given by reference to an imaginary coordinate system based on lines of **longitude** and lines of **latitude**. *Longitude corresponds to the x-numbers, and latitude to the y-numbers in the Cartesian coordinate system.*

grid references as used on maps are a **Cartesian coordinate** system.

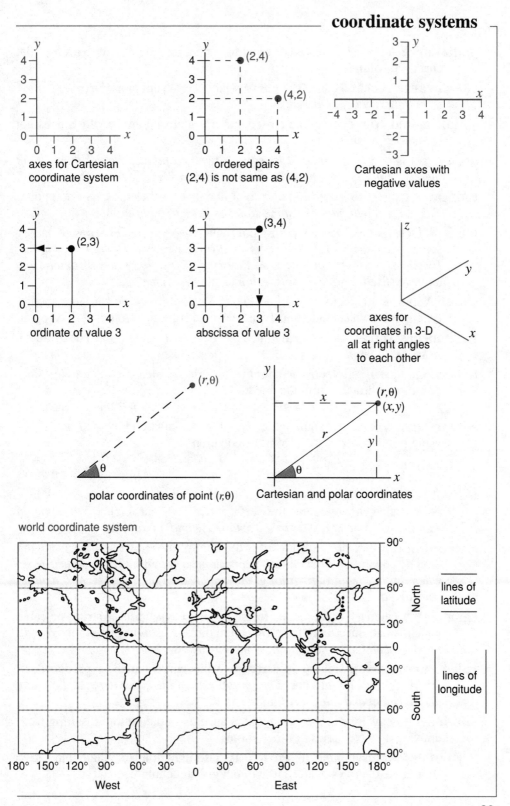

axes for Cartesian
coordinate system

ordered pairs
(2,4) is not same as (4,2)

Cartesian axes with
negative values

ordinate of value 3

abscissa of value 3

axes for
coordinates in 3-D
all at right angles
to each other

polar coordinates of point (r, θ)

Cartesian and polar coordinates

world coordinate system

lines of
latitude

lines of
longitude

North

South

90° 60° 30° 0 30° 60° 90°

180° 150° 120° 90° 60° 30° 0 30° 60° 90° 120° 150° 180°

West   East

plane curve A plane curve is a **curve** whose entire length lies within a single flat surface or **plane**.

closed curve A closed curve is a **curve** which has NO end points. *No beginning or ending can be identified.*

simple closed curve A simple closed curve is a **closed curve** which does not cross itself at any point.

arc An arc is part of a **curve**. *It must have two end points, though these might merely be marked to show the arc as part of a bigger curve.*

tangent A tangent to a **curve** is a straight line that touches the curve at a point. *The tangent will have the same slope as the curve at that point.*

locus A locus is the line of a path along which a point moves so as to satisfy some given conditions. *A locus is usually a curve but does not have to be. Example: A point that moves so that it is always the same distance from another (fixed) point will follow a locus in the shape of a circle.*

spiral A spiral is the **locus** of a point moving in the plane of, and around, another (fixed) point while continuously increasing its distance from that fixed point.

Archimedes' spiral is the **spiral** which can be drawn, using **polar coordinates**, from the equation $r = a\theta$ (a is a constant $\neq 0$, θ is in radians)

hyperbolic spiral A hyperbolic spiral is the **spiral** which can be drawn, using **polar coordinates**, from the equation
$$r = a \div \theta \qquad (a \text{ is a constant} \neq 0, \theta \text{ is in radians})$$

equiangular spiral An equiangular spiral is the **spiral** which can be drawn, using **polar coordinates**, from the equation
$$r = ae^{k\theta} \qquad (a, k \text{ are constants} \neq 0, \theta \text{ is in radians})$$
$$(e \approx 2.7182818)$$

helix A helix is the shape drawn on the curved surface of a cylinder or cone by a point which moves along the surface at a constant angle. *Two common examples of a helix are a circular staircase and a corkscrew.*

curve of pursuit A curve of pursuit is the line followed by one object moving directly toward another object which is also moving. *The simplest case, when both are moving along the same straight line, is not usually considered.*

catenary A catenary is the curve formed by a heavy uniform string or cable which is hanging freely from two end points. *It is most commonly seen in the overhead cables used to transmit electricity.*

ruled curve A ruled curve is a recognizable curve which is produced by drawing only straight lines. *The smoothness of the curve depends upon the arrangement and number of lines drawn.*

envelope An envelope is the curve which appears as the outline resulting from drawing a whole series of other curves.

asymptote An asymptote to a curve is a straight line to which the curve continuously draws nearer but without ever touching it.

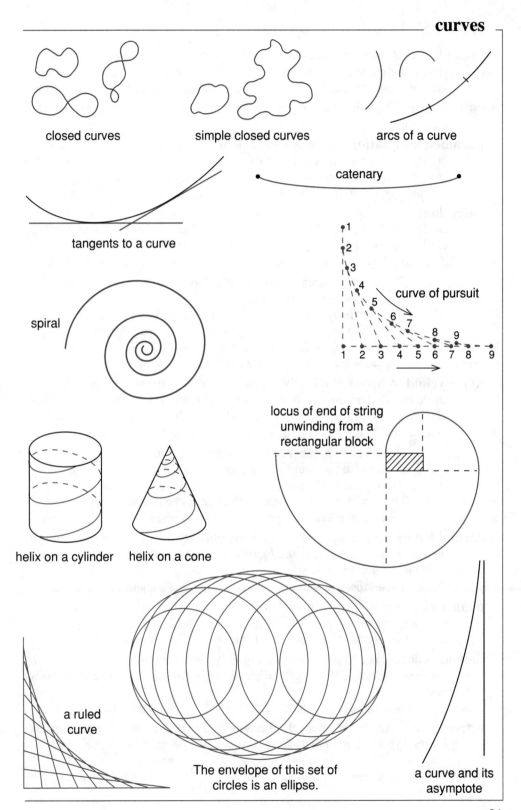

closed curves

simple closed curves

arcs of a curve

catenary

tangents to a curve

spiral

curve of pursuit

locus of end of string
unwinding from a
rectangular block

helix on a cylinder   helix on a cone

a ruled
curve

The envelope of this set of
circles is an ellipse.

a curve and its
asymptote

cycloid A cycloid is the **locus** of a single point on a circle when that circle is rolled along a straight line. *A complete turn of the circle makes one arch.*
Area between one arch and the line = $3\pi a^2$ Length of one arch = $8a$ (a = radius)

cusp A cusp is a point on a curve where the curve makes a complete reversal of direction.

parametric equations are those that link two (or more) variables, not directly, but by expressing them in terms of equations using another variable that is common to all the equations. *Examples are given below for the epicycloid and the hypocycloid where coordinates are given in terms of the variable θ.*

epicycloid An epicycloid is the **locus** of a single point on a circle when that circle is rolled around the OUTSIDE of another circle known as the base circle. *The exact shape of this curve, and the number of cusps it has, will be determined by the relative sizes of the rolling circle and the base circle.*

> The x, y coordinates needed to plot an epicycloid are given by the **parametric equations**:
> $$x = a(n \cos \theta - \cos n\theta) \qquad y = a(n \sin \theta - \sin n\theta)$$
> θ may take any values (normally in the range $0°$ to $360°$)
> If n is a whole number, then there will be $(n - 1)$ cusps.
> The value of a changes the size of the curve.

hypocycloid A hypocycloid is the **locus** of a single point on a circle when that circle is rolled around the INSIDE of another circle known as the base circle. *The exact shape of this curve, and the number of cusps it has, will be determined by the relative sizes of the rolling circle and the base circle.*

> The x, y coordinates needed to plot an epicycloid are given by the **parametric equations**:
> $$x = a(n \cos \theta + \cos n\theta) \qquad y = a(n \sin \theta - \sin n\theta)$$
> The same remarks apply as for the epicyloid equations above except that in this case there will be $(n + 1)$ cusps.

cardioid A cardioid is an **epicycloid** having only ONE **cusp**. *In the equations for the epicycloid, $n = 2$. It is the locus drawn when the rolling circle and the base circle are the same size.*
> Area enclosed by cardioid = $6\pi a^2$ Perimeter length = $16a$

nephroid A nephroid is an **epicycloid** having only TWO **cusps**. *In the equations for the epicycloid, $n = 3$. The rolling circle is half the size of the base circle.*
> Area enclosed by nephroid = $12\pi a^2$ Perimeter length = $24a$

deltoid A deltoid is a **hypocycloid** having only THREE **cusps**. *In the equations for the hypocycloid, $n = 2$. The rolling circle is one-third the size of the base circle.*
> Area enclosed by deltoid = $2\pi a^2$ Perimeter length = $16a$

astroid An astroid is a **hypocycloid** having only FOUR **cusps**. *In the equations for the hypocycloid, $n = 3$. The equations can be rewritten more simply as:*
> $$x = 4a \cos^3 \theta \qquad\qquad y = 4a \sin^3 \theta$$
> Area enclosed by astroid = $\frac{3}{8}\pi a^2$ Perimeter length = $6a$

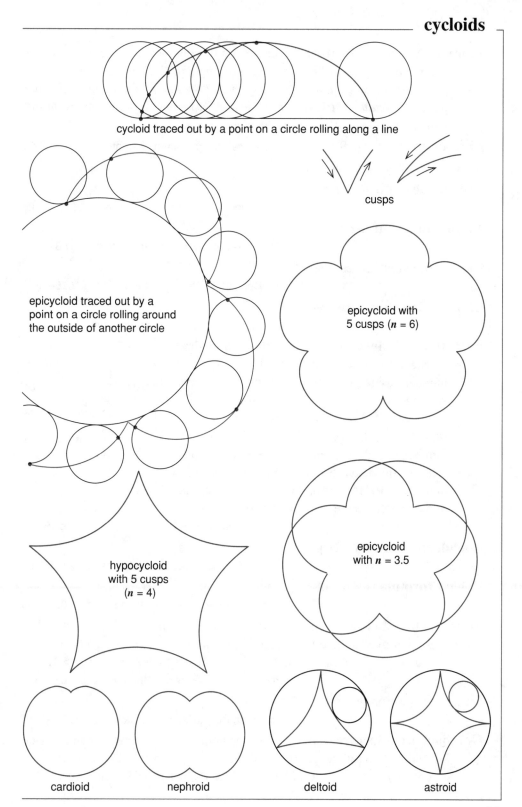

cycloid traced out by a point on a circle rolling along a line

cusps

epicycloid traced out by a
point on a circle rolling around
the outside of another circle

epicycloid with
5 cusps ($n = 6$)

hypocycloid
with 5 cusps
($n = 4$)

epicycloid
with $n = 3.5$

cardioid

nephroid

deltoid

astroid

eponym An eponym is EITHER the name of a person, factual or fictitious, which is used to form a word or phrase identifying a particular thing, OR the thing itself. *The person's name is usually that of the one first associated in some way with whatever is being identified. Apart from the eponyms explained here, others are dealt with on the pages given.*

Abelian group *see* p. 99   Niels Abel, Norwegian mathematician, 1802–1829

Archimedean solids *see* p. 74

Archimedes' spiral *see* p. 30

Archimedes, Greek mathematician, c.287–212 BC

Argand diagram *see* p. 67

Jean Robert Argand, Swiss mathematician, 1768–1822

Cartesian coordinates *see* p. 28

Rene Descartes, French mathematician, 1596–1650

Diophantine equations *see* p. 9

Diophantus, Greek mathematician, 1802–1829

Eratosthenes' sieve is an **algorithm** for finding **prime numbers**. First write down as many numbers as required to be searched, in order starting with 1 and not skipping any. Cross out 1. Leave 2 and cross out every second number (4, 6, 8, etc.). Leave 3 and cross out every third number (6, 9, 12, etc.). Since 4 is already crossed out, leave 5 and cross out every fifth number (10, 15, etc.). When complete, the numbers left are the prime numbers.

1̶	2	3	4̶	5	6̶
7	8̶	9̶	1̶0̶	11	1̶2̶
13	1̶4̶	1̶5̶	1̶6̶	17	1̶8̶
19	2̶0̶	2̶1̶	2̶2̶	23	2̶4̶
2̶5̶	2̶6̶	2̶7̶	2̶8̶	29	3̶0̶
31	3̶2̶	3̶3̶	3̶4̶	3̶5̶	3̶6̶
37	3̶8̶	3̶9̶	4̶0̶	41	4̶2̶
43	4̶4̶	4̶5̶	4̶6̶	47	4̶8̶
4̶9̶	5̶0̶	5̶1̶			

Eratosthenes, Greek astronomer, c.276–c.196 BC

Euclidean geometry *see* p. 42

Euclid, Greek mathematician, c.325 BC

Euler's formula *see* p. 108

Leonhard Euler, Swiss mathematician, 1707–1783

Fermat's last theorem The most famous theorem in mathematics, though it was not proved until 1994, is that the equation $x^n + y^n = z^n$ has no solutions in whole numbers for x, y, and z if n is greater than 2 and $x, y, z > 1$.

Pierre de Fermat, French mathematician, 1601–1665

Fibonacci sequence *see* p. 84

Leonardo Fibonacci, Italian mathematician, c.1170–1240

Goldbach's conjecture is that every even number from 6 onward can be made by adding two **prime numbers**. There are often several possibilities.

Christian Goldbach, Russian mathematician, 1690–1764

Hamiltonian walk A Hamiltonian walk is a path traced out on a **topological graph** which visits every vertex once and once only, except possibly for the start and finish, which might be on the same vertex.

Sir William Hamilton, Irish mathematician, 1805–1865

Jordan curve ≡ **simple closed curve**

Camille Jordan, French mathematician, 1838–1922

Lucas sequence *see* p. 84

François E. A. Lucas, French mathematician, 1842–1891

Mersenne primes are those **prime numbers** that can be made from the expression $2^n - 1$. This method for generating prime numbers works only when n itself is prime, but not always even then. For instance, it works when $n = 2, 3, 5$, or 7 but not when $n = 11$, and not when $n = 23$ as well as several other prime values.

Marin Mersenne, French mathematician, 1588–1648

Möbius band or strip A Möbius band is made by taking a rectangular strip of paper like that shown as ABCD and fastening the two shorter edges together (AB and CD) but, before fastening, giving the strip a half twist so that A fastens to D and B to C. The strange property of this band is that it now has only 1 edge and 1 side.

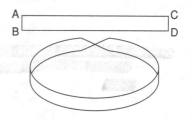

August Möbius, German mathematician, 1790–1868

Napier's rods or bones *see* p. 21

John Napier, Scottish mathematician, 1550–1617

Pascal's triangle is an array of numbers, in the shape of a triangle, having a 1 at the top and also at the ends of each line. All the other numbers are made by adding the pair of numbers closest to them in the line above.

```
            1
          1   1
        1   2   1
      1   3   3   1
    1   4   6   4   1
  1   5  10  10   5   1
1   6  15  20  15   6   1
1  7  21  35  35  21   7   1
```

Examples: 1 + 4   4 + 6   6 + 4   4 + 1
*   =5   =10   =10   =5*

Blaise Pascal, French mathematician, 1550–1617

Platonic solids *see* p. 74

Plato, Greek philosopher, c.427–c.347 BC

Pythagoras' theorem *see* p. 114

Pythagoras, Greek mathematician, c.580–c.500 BC

Ramanujan's formula *see* p. 26 (under **ellipse**).

Srinivasa Ramanujan, Hindu mathematician, 1887–1920

Simpson's rule *see* p. 105

Thomas Simpson, English mathematician, 1710–1761

Venn diagrams *see* p. 87   John Venn, English mathematician, 1834–1923

factors, multiples, and primes

Number, as used in this section, means only a **whole number**.

factor A factor is a **number** which divides exactly into another **number**. *Thus 1 is a factor of every number and every number is a factor of itself. A number can have several factors, as shown in the table opposite.*
Examples: *1 is a factor of 5;*   *3 is a factor of 6;*   *4 is a factor of 12*
           7 is a factor of 7;   *2 and 17 are factors of 68*

proper factors The proper factors of a number are all its **factors** EXCEPT for the number itself.
Examples: *The factors of 12 are 1, 2, 3, 4, 6, and 12, but its proper factors are only 1, 2, 3, 4, and 6*
           The proper factors of 20 are 1, 2, 4, 5, and 10

proper divisors ≡ proper factors

common factors are those **factors** shared by two (or more) numbers.
Example: *12 has 1, 2, 3, 4, 6, 12 as factors*
         18 has 1, 2, 3, 6, 9, 18 as factors
         So the common factors of 12 and 18 are 1, 2, 3, 6

greatest common factor (gcf) The highest common factor of two (or more) numbers is the **common factor** of all those numbers which has the greatest value. *In some cases the gcf may be 1 or one of the actual numbers.*
Examples: *From the previous example, the gcf of 12 and 18 is 6*
         The gcf of 12 and 17 is 1   *The gcf of 5,15, 30 is 5*

prime number A prime number is a number having two, and only two, **factors**. *The list opposite gives the first 160 prime numbers. The list could continue forever. Note that 1 is NOT a prime number, since it has only one factor.*

prime factors The prime factors of a number are all those **factors** of the number which are themselves **prime numbers**. *A prime number has only one prime factor: itself.*
Example: *All the factors of 12 are 1, 2, 3, 4, 6, and 12 but its only prime factors are 2 and 3*

composite number A composite number must have three or more **factors**. *It cannot be 0 or 1 or a prime number.*
Examples: *4, 6, 8, 9, 10, 12, 15 are all composite numbers.*

multiple A multiple is a number made by multiplying together two other numbers. *A number is a multiple of any of its factors.*
Example: *12 is a multiple of 2, since 12 = 2 × 6*

least common multiple (lcm) The least (or lowest) common multiple of two (or more) numbers is the smallest possible number into which ALL of them will divide. *Example: The lcm of 3, 4, and 8 is 24*

fundamental theorem of arithmetic Any composite number can be made by multiplying together a set of prime numbers, and this can be done in only one way. *The reordering of the prime numbers is not considered as different.*
Examples: *12 = 2 × 2 × 3, which in exponent form is $2^2 × 3$*
         126 = 2 × 3 × 3 × 7 or $2 × 3^2 × 7$

factors, multiples, and primes

Number and factors

Number	Factors
1	1
2	1, 2
3	1, 3
4	1, 2, 4
5	1, 5
6	1, 2, 3, 6
7	1, 7
8	1, 2, 4, 8
9	1, 3, 9
10	1, 2, 5, 10
11	1, 11
12	1, 2, 3, 4, 6, 12
13	1, 13
14	1, 2, 7, 14
15	1, 3, 5, 15
16	1, 2, 4, 8, 16
17	1, 17
18	1, 2, 3, 6, 9, 18
19	1, 19
20	1, 2, 4, 5, 10, 20
21	1, 3, 7, 21
22	1, 2, 11, 22
23	1, 23
24	1, 2, 3, 4, 6, 8, 12, 24
25	1, 5, 25
26	1, 2, 13, 26
27	1, 3, 9, 27
28	1, 2, 4, 7, 14, 28
29	1, 29
30	1, 2, 3, 5, 6, 10, 15, 30
31	1, 31
32	1, 2, 4, 8, 16, 32
33	1, 3, 11, 33
34	1, 2, 17, 34
35	1, 5, 7, 35
36	1, 2, 4, 6, 9, 18, 36
37	1, 37
38	1, 2, 19, 38
39	1, 3, 13, 39
40	1, 2, 4, 5, 8, 10, 20, 40

Prime number list

2	179	419	661
3	181	421	673
5	191	431	677
7	193	433	683
11	197	439	691
13	199	443	701
17	211	449	709
19	223	457	719
23	227	461	727
29	229	463	733
31	233	467	739
37	239	479	743
41	241	487	751
43	251	491	757
47	257	499	761
53	263	503	769
59	269	509	773
61	271	521	787
67	277	523	797
71	281	541	809
73	283	547	811
79	293	557	821
83	307	563	823
89	311	569	827
97	313	571	829
101	317	577	839
103	331	587	853
107	337	593	857
109	347	599	859
113	349	601	863
127	353	607	877
131	359	613	881
137	367	617	883
139	373	619	887
149	379	631	907
151	383	641	911
157	389	643	919
163	397	647	929
167	401	653	937
173	409	659	941

formulas for shapes

rectangle

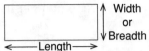

Area = Length × Width

Perimeter = 2 × (Length + Width)

parallelogram

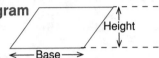

Area = Base × Height

trapezoid

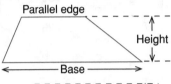

Area = (Base + Parallel edge) × Height ÷ 2

triangle

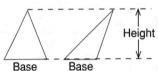

Area = Base × Height ÷ 2

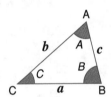

Law of sines: $\dfrac{a}{\sin A} = \dfrac{b}{\sin B} = \dfrac{c}{\sin C}$

Law of cosines: $a^2 = b^2 + c^2 - 2bc \cos A$
$\cos A = (b^2 + c^2 - a^2) \div 2bc$

a, b, c are the lengths of the edges
s is the length of the semiperimeter
$s = (a + b + c) \div 2$

Area = $\sqrt{s(s-a)(s-b)(s-c)}$

circle

Area = π × Radius × Radius = πr^2 or $\pi d^2 \div 4$

Circumference = 2 × π × Radius
= π × Diameter = πd

arc of a circle

Length of arc = Central angle (in degrees) ÷ 360 × Circumference of full circle

$= \dfrac{\theta}{360°} \times 2\pi r$

sector of a circle

Area of sector = Central angle (in degrees) ÷ 360 × Area of full circle

$= \dfrac{\theta}{360°} \times 2\pi r^2$

segment of a circle

Area of segment $= \left(\dfrac{\pi \times \theta}{360} - \dfrac{\sin \theta}{2} \right) \times r^2$

chord of a circle

Length of chord $= 2\,r \sin\left(\dfrac{\theta}{2}\right)$

ellipse

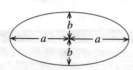

Area of ellipse $= \pi\,a\,b$

Circumference $= \pi(a + b)$ (first approximation)

or $\pi[3(a + b) - \sqrt{(a + 3b)(3a + b)}]$

(better approximation)

cylinder

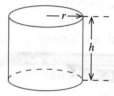

Volume $= \pi \times$ Radius $\times$ Radius $\times$ Height $= \pi r^2 h$

Curved surface area $= 2 \times \pi \times$ Radius $\times$ Height

$= 2\pi r h$

Total surface area $= 2\pi r\,(r + h)$

cone

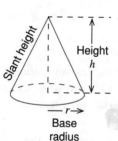

Volume $= \frac{1}{3} \times$ Area of base $\times$ Height

$= \pi r^2 h \div 3$

Curved surface area

$= \pi \times$ Radius of base $\times$ Slant height

Slant height $= \sqrt{r^2 + h^2}$

sphere

Volume $= 4 \times \pi \times$ (Radius)$^3 \div 3 = \pi \times$ (Diameter)$^3 \div 6$

Surface area $= 4 \times \pi \times$ (Radius)$^2 = \pi \times$ (Diameter)^2

pyramid

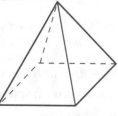

Volume $= \frac{1}{3} \times$ Area of base $\times$ Height

frustum

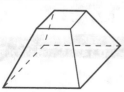

Volume $= (\,A + B + \sqrt{A \times B}\,) \times h \div 3$
where A and B are the areas of
the top and bottom parallel faces
and h is the perpendicular
distance between them

fractions

fraction A fraction is a measure of how something is to be divided up or shared out. *There are four principal ways of expressing fractions: common, decimal, percentage, and ratio.*

common fraction A common fraction is a **fraction** written in the form of two whole numbers, one above the other, separated by a line. The bottom number must not be a 1 or zero. *It represents a division to be done, where the upper number is to be divided by the bottom.*
Examples: $\frac{1}{2}$ $\frac{3}{4}$ $\frac{2}{3}$ $\frac{99}{150}$ $\frac{-1}{4}$

numerator The numerator is the top number in a **common fraction**.

denominator The denominator is the bottom number in a **common fraction**.
Example: In the fraction $\frac{8}{9}$, 8 is the numerator, 9 is the denominator.

least common denominator or **lcd** The least (or lowest) common denominator of two (or more) fractions is the smallest number into which all their **denominators** will divide. *It is the lcm of the denominators.*
Example: For the fractions $\frac{2}{3}$ $\frac{1}{8}$ $\frac{5}{6}$ their lcd is 24.

proper fraction A proper fraction is a **common fraction** in which the **numerator** *(= top number)* is smaller than the **denominator** *(= bottom number).*

improper fraction An improper fraction is a **common fraction** in which the **numerator** *(= top number)* is larger than the **denominator** *(= bottom number).*
Examples: $\frac{9}{8}$ $\frac{4}{3}$ $\frac{100}{17}$ *are all improper fractions.*

mixed number A mixed number is made up of two parts: a whole number followed by a **proper fraction**.
Examples: $1\frac{1}{2}$ $5\frac{7}{8}$ $-2\frac{5}{6}$ *are all mixed numbers.*

decimal fraction A decimal fraction is a way of expressing values of fractions less than 1 using the normal **decimal place value system** extended to the right of the units column so as to give values of $\frac{1}{10}$, $\frac{1}{100}$, etc.
Example: 0.376 *means* $\frac{3}{10} + \frac{7}{100} + \frac{6}{1000} = \frac{376}{1000}$

decimal point A decimal point is a dot used to show that the values which follow make up a **decimal fraction**. *A comma is used in the metric and SI systems.*

repeating decimal A repeating decimal is a **decimal fraction** which goes on REPEATING itself without end.
Examples: 0.3333333 …   *usually written* $0.\overline{3}$
0.14285714285714285714 …   *usually written* $0.\overline{142857}$
where the bar above the number shows what is to be repeated; it may be either a single digit or a block of digits.

terminating decimal A terminating decimal is a **decimal fraction** that ends after a definite number of digits have been given.
Examples: 0.5   0.123   0.67   0.747474

periodic decimal ≡ **repeating decimal**. *Its period is the number of digits which are repeated each time.*   *Example:* $0.\overline{142857}$ *has a period of 6*

percent indicates a special type of **fraction** in which the value given is a measure of the number of parts in every 100 parts that is to be used.
Example: 25 percent means 25 in every 100 or $\frac{25}{100}$

% = percent   *Example: 75% is 75 percent, which is $\frac{75}{100}$*

ratio is used to compare the sizes of two (or more) quantities.
Example: Mortar for building a brick wall is made by mixing 2 parts of cement to 7 parts of sand. (The parts may be decided by weight or by volume, just so long as the same units are used.) Then it can be said that the ratio of cement to sand is 2 to 7, which is also written in the form 2:7

equivalent fractions are two, or more, fractions that have the same value but are different in form.
Example: The set of fractions $\frac{3}{4}$ $\frac{6}{8}$ $\frac{63}{84}$ 75%   0.75

all look different, but they all have the same effect in use.

Table of values of some equivalent fractions					
common fraction	decimal fraction	%	common fraction	decimal fraction	%
$\frac{1}{20}$	0.05	5	$\frac{5}{10}$ $\frac{1}{2}$	0.5	50
$\frac{1}{10}$	0.1	10	$\frac{6}{10}$ $\frac{3}{5}$	0.6	60
$\frac{2}{10}$ $\frac{1}{5}$	0.2	20	$\frac{2}{3}$	0.666...	$66\frac{2}{3}$
$\frac{1}{4}$	0.25	25	$\frac{7}{10}$	0.7	70
$\frac{3}{10}$	0.3	30	$\frac{3}{4}$	0.75	75
$\frac{1}{3}$	0.333...	$33\frac{1}{3}$	$\frac{8}{10}$ $\frac{4}{5}$	0.8	80
$\frac{4}{10}$ $\frac{2}{5}$	0.4	40	$\frac{9}{10}$	0.9	90

To change a **common fraction** into a **decimal fraction**, divide the top number by the bottom.
Example: To change $\frac{3}{7}$ work out 3 ÷ 7 = 0.428 571 …

To change a **decimal fraction** into a **percentage**, multiply it by 100
Example: To change 0.428571 work out 0.428 571 × 100 = 42.8571%

To change a **common fraction** into a **percentage**, do both the above in that order.
Example: To change $\frac{3}{7}$ work out 3 ÷ 7 × 100 = 42.8571 …%

reduced fraction A reduced fraction is a **common fraction** in its simplest possible form. *To get this, divide both the top and bottom numbers of the fraction by the SAME VALUE until it becomes impossible to do so anymore.*
Example: To reduce $\frac{150}{240}$ divide both by 10 to get $\frac{15}{24}$,

then divide both by 3 to get $\frac{5}{8}$

algebraic fractions are rather like **common fractions** in their form, but use algebraic expressions for their numerator and/or denominator.
Examples: $\frac{a}{b}$ $\frac{x+y}{3x-y}$ $\frac{3(x+y)(x-y)}{8(x^2+y)}$

geometry is the study of the properties and relationships of **points, lines**, and **surfaces** in space.

plane geometry is **geometry** confined to two-dimensional space only.

Euclidean geometry is the **geometry** that keeps within the rules as laid down by Euclid. *It is what is usually meant when the word "geometry" is used without any other descriptor. It is also the geometry which is most often used in the ordinary, everyday world.*

point A point indicates a position only and has no size. *In a drawing it must have some size in order to be seen, but in any work involving a point its size is ignored. It has no dimensions.*

line A line is the path followed by a **point** when it moves from one position to another so that it has a measurable size (its length) only along that path. *The drawing of a line requires that it has some width in order to be seen, but this size is ignored in all work that would be affected by it. It has only one dimension.*

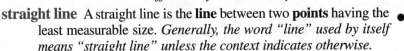

straight line A straight line is the **line** between two **points** having the least measurable size. *Generally, the word "line" used by itself means "straight line" unless the context indicates otherwise.*

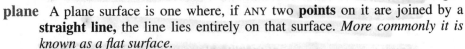

linear is used to indicate an association with a straight line.

line segment A line segment is a piece of a **straight line**. *Strictly speaking, a straight line is fixed by two separate points and goes on indefinitely in both directions so that it cannot be measured. It is only the line segment which is measurable. The single word "line" is usually taken to mean "line segment."*

surface A surface is the two-dimensional outer boundary (or skin) of a three-dimensional object. *It follows next in order after point and line so that now sizes can be measured in two dimensions. A surface is considered to have* NO *thickness.*

plane A plane surface is one where, if ANY two **points** on it are joined by a **straight line,** the line lies entirely on that surface. *More commonly it is known as a flat surface.*

parallel Two (or more) **lines**, which must lie in the same **plane**, are said to be parallel if, no matter how far they are extended in either direction, they are always the same distance apart. *Usually this is applied only to straight lines, but it can be applied to curves that remain a constant distance apart.*

perpendicular Two **straight lines** (or **planes**) are said to be perpendicular to each other if, at their crossing or meeting, a right angle is formed.

orthogonal ≡ **perpendicular**.

collinear Three, or more, **points** are said to be collinear if one **straight line** can be drawn which passes through ALL of them.

vertical angles When two **straight lines** cross each other, four angles are made; any pair of these which touch each other only at the crossing point are vertical angles. *Vertical angles are equal in size.*

adjacent angles When two **straight lines** cross each other, four angles are made; any pair of these which touch each other along a line are adjacent angles. *Adjacent angles add up to 180°.*

transversal A transversal is a straight line that cuts across other straight lines. *The other lines are usually parallel.*

alternate angles When a **transversal** cuts two **parallel** lines, alternate angles are any pair of angles that lie on OPPOSITE sides of the transversal and on OPPOSITE relative sides of the parallel lines. *Alternate angles are equal in size. They are also known as Z-angles.*

corresponding angles When a **transversal** cuts two **parallel** lines, corresponding angles are any pair of angles which lie on the SAME sides of the transversal and on the SAME relative sides of the parallel lines. *Corresponding angles are equal in size.*

similar Geometrical figures are said to be similar if they are the SAME in shape but DIFFERENT in size. *One shape is an enlargement of another. Corresponding angles in each shape will be the same size. All these triangles are similar:*

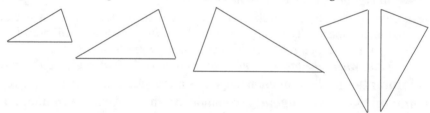

congruent Geometrical figures are said to be congruent if they are the SAME in shape AND size. *One shape can be fitted exactly over the other, being turned around and/or over as necessary. Such shapes can also be described as being identical. These four triangles are all congruent:*

vertical A vertical line at any point on the earth is the **straight line** which would join that point to the center of the earth. *Usually, in drawings, a vertical line means one which goes in the top-to-bottom direction of the page.*

horizontal A horizontal line at any point on the earth is a **straight line** that lies at right angles to the vertical at that point. *It is often described as "level." Usually, in drawings, a horizontal line means one which goes across the page.*

geometry of the circle

angle properties of circles is a collection of theorems which give the relationships among various parts of a circle (chord, segment, etc.) and angles associated with them.

subtended angle Given three distinct points A, B, and C (which are not in a straight line), the subtended angle of any two of the points at the third is the angle formed between the lines drawn from the first two points to the third. *The subtended angle of points A and C at B would be the angle formed between the lines BA and BC.*
Example: The angle subtended by the diameter of the moon at any point on the earth is about half a degree.

angle inscribed The angle inscribed in a segment is the angle formed between the two lines drawn from the ends of the **chord** making the **segment** to any point on the circumference of that segment. *It is the angle subtended at the point on the circumference by the chord. In any given segment all the subtended angles are the same size.*

angle inscribed in a semicircle In any semicircle the angle **subtended** by the diameter at any point on the circumference is a right angle.

central angle The central angle of a circle is the one formed between the two radii drawn from two points on the circumference. *It is the angle subtended at the center by the chord defined by those two points. Given any chord, the angle it subtends at the center is twice the angle in the segment which is on the same side of the chord as the center.*

tangent A tangent to a circle is a line which, no matter how far it is extended, touches the circle at one point only. *From any one fixed point outside a circle two tangents can always be drawn to that circle. The radius drawn at the point where the tangent touches the circle is at right angles to the tangent.*

common tangent A common tangent is a **tangent** that touches two circles.

common external tangent A common external tangent is a **common tangent** that DOES NOT pass between the centers of the two circles.

common internal tangent A common internal tangent is a **common tangent** that DOES pass between the centers of the two circles.

secant A secant is a line which cuts across a circle at two points. *A tangent can be considered a special case of a secant in which the two cuts are coincident.*

alternate segments Any **chord** drawn in a circle creates two segments, and one is said to be the alternate of the other. *When a chord is drawn from the point of contact of a tangent, then the angle between the tangent and the chord, measured on ONE side of the chord, is equal to the angle inscribed in the alternate segment, which lies on the OTHER side of the chord.*

intersecting chords are two **chords** drawn in the same circle which cross at some point. *If the two chords are labeled as AB and CD and they cross at O, then $OA \times OB = OC \times OD$. In the case where O is outside the circle with OT a tangent and OAB a secant to that circle, then $OA \times OB = (OT)^2$*

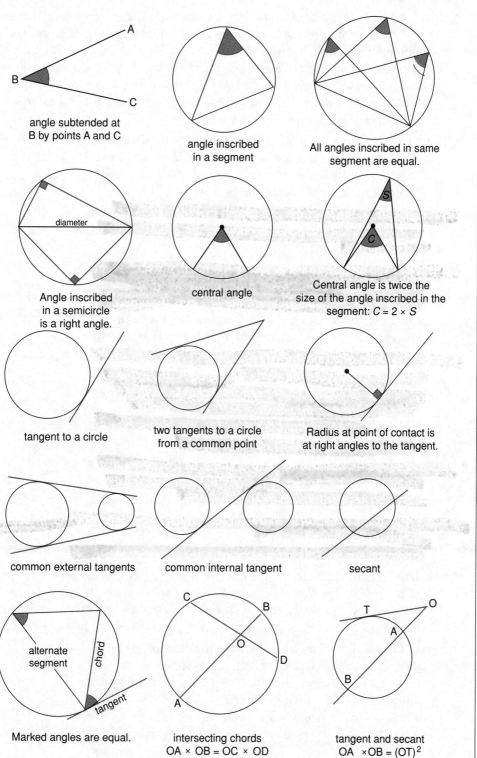

angle subtended at
B by points A and C

angle inscribed
in a segment

All angles inscribed in same
segment are equal.

Angle inscribed
in a semicircle
is a right angle.

central angle

Central angle is twice the
size of the angle inscribed in the
segment: $C = 2 \times S$

tangent to a circle

two tangents to a circle
from a common point

Radius at point of contact is
at right angles to the tangent.

common external tangents

common internal tangent

secant

Marked angles are equal.

intersecting chords
$OA \times OB = OC \times OD$

tangent and secant
$OA \times OB = (OT)^2$

graph A graph is a diagram showing EITHER the relationship between some variable quantities OR the connections that exist between a set of points (as in **topology**). *The word "graph" on its own usually means the first kind, where the relationship is shown by means of points plotted on a coordinate system, and is the type covered in this section. Statistical graphs are also of the first kind but are usually named by type: bar chart, pictogram, etc. For most work the relationship concerns only two quantities.*

quadrants The two axes of a coordinate system divide the plane into four separate sections known as quadrants. These are identified as the first, second, third, and fourth quadrants in the way shown on the right.

second 2nd	first 1st
third 3rd	fourth 4th

linear graph A linear graph is a **graph** in which all the points representing the relationship between the quantities lie on a straight line.

intercept The intercept of a **graph** is the point at which it cuts across an axis. *For linear graphs this word is usually reserved for the point at which the line cuts the y-axis. Example: In the linear graph shown on the right the intercept is ⁻2. The y-intercept is usually designated by b.*

slope The slope of a line drawn on a **graph** is a measure of its inclination relative to the *x*-axis. *This is expressed as the ratio of its vertical change to its horizontal change, both changes being measured on the scales of their respective axes. Example: In the diagram the slope is given by a ÷ b and is positive, since y INCREASES as x increases.*

negative slope A negative slope is a **slope** which shows that *y* DECREASES as *x* increases. *It is measured as for slope (above) but has a negative sign in front of the value.*

$y = mx + b$ is the equation of a straight line which has a **slope** of value *m* and an **intercept** (on the y-axis) at *b*. *Example: y = 3x – 4 has a slope of 3 and an intercept of ⁻4*

trend line A trend line is the single line that best represents the general direction of a set of points. *This is especially useful when some observed data has been plotted that does not lie on a straight line, but estimates are required to be made on the basis of that data. It is also known as a* **line of best fit.**

interpolation An interpolation is an estimation of the likely value of an unknown piece of data, falling WITHIN the range of some known data and based on the evidence provided by that known data. *This usually involves using the trend line. Example: In the graph on the right the values of the known data are shown by black dots, and the interpolated value by a red dot.*

extrapolation An extrapolation is an estimation of the likely value of an unknown piece of data, falling OUTSIDE the range of some known data and based on the evidence provided by that known data. *This usually involves using the trend line. Example: In the graph on the right the values of the known data are shown by black dots, and the extrapolated value by a red dot.*

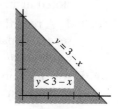

quadratic graph A quadratic graph is a **graph** in which the relationship between the variables is given by a **quadratic equation**. *Its shape is that of a parabola. Examples:*

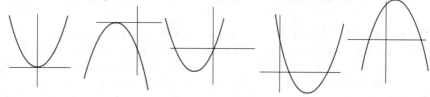

roots of a quadratic The two **roots** of a **quadratic expression**, when it is drawn as a graph, are indicated by the points at which the line of the graph crosses the x-axis. *If the line crosses the x-axis, the two x-values at those crossings are the roots of that quadratic. If the line touches, but does not cross, the x-axis, the two roots are equal. If the line does not cross or touch the x-axis, the roots are complex numbers. Example: The graph on the right of the quadratic* $x^2 - x - 2$ *has its roots at* $^-1$ *and 2*

cubic A cubic graph is a **graph** in which the relationship between the variables involves an expression of **degree** 3
Example: The graph of $y = x^3 - 4x^2 - 15x + 18$ *is shown on the right. Its roots are* $^-3$, *1, and 6*

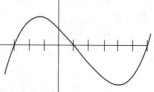

inverse square An inverse square relationship is $y = k/x^2$, where k can be any number. *A graph showing this relationship has a general shape like that shown on the right. If k is negative, then the graph will be rotated into the fourth quadrant.*

exponential An exponential graph is a **graph** in which the relationship between the variables involves an expression in which one of the variables appears as an **exponent**. *The word is often used in connection with "exponential growth" to indicate that its rate of change is always increasing. Example:* $y = 2^x$ *is an exponential relationship.*

inequalities An inequality is shown by an expression such as $y < 3 - x$, meaning that y can take any value which is LESS THAN that of $3 - x$. *This is shown on a graph by drawing the line of* $y = 3 - x$ *and shading the region where y is always less than that.*

$y = 3 - x$

$y < 3 - x$

information technology includes a whole range of electronic devices and techniques used in collecting, storing, retrieving, processing, presenting, and transmitting data. *Computer systems are usually a major item in all these activities, but are not exclusively so.*

computer A computer is a machine which will perform any operations that can be expressed in terms of logic and arithmetic. *Its power (and its usefulness) lies in the speed at which it works. Modern computers are capable of carrying out over 300 million instructions in every second.*

program A program is the set of instructions, written in a particular language which a **computer** can understand, to tell the computer exactly how the required operations are to be done.

programming language A programming language consists of a set of precisely defined rules, and the exact way in which they are to be written, so as to be understood by a computer. *There are several different languages, each written for some specific purpose.*

BASIC stands for **B**eginners **A**ll-purpose **S**ymbolic **I**nstruction **C**ode. This is a **programming language** originally developed for educational purposes that is being continually extended for use in commercial applications.

C and **C++** are both **programming languages**, C++ being an extension of C. These are among the languages most widely used by professional programmers.

Logo is a **programming language** developed for educational use.

RAM stands for **R**andom **A**ccess **M**emory. This is an electronic store for information which can be written to, or read by, the computer system. The information is LOST when the power is switched off.

ROM stands for **R**ead **O**nly **M**emory. This is an electronic store for information which can be read by, but NOT written to, the computer system. The information is NOT LOST when the power is off.

bit A bit is the smallest piece of information that can be stored or transmitted electronically. It can be represented by a 0 or a 1.

byte A byte is a number of **bits** grouped together to make up a single unit of information. Common usage has 1 byte = 8 bits, so that a byte could be 01001110, which is the binary representation of the number 78.

Kb stands for **K**ilobyte, which is 2^{10} or 1024 **bytes**.

Mb stands for **M**egabyte, which is 2^{20} or 1048 576 **bytes**.

Gb stands for **G**igabyte, which is 2^{30} or 1073 741 824 **bytes**.

database A database is a computer program which allows information to be stored in an organized way so that each separate item can easily be found.

record A record is one set of information in a **database** which is made up of several separate pieces of data linked together by a common theme. *For example, all the information about one person could form a record.*

field A field is one specific piece of information in a **database**, and a collection of fields on a common theme form a **record**.

spreadsheet A spreadsheet is a computer program which presents the user with a large number of cells (like squared paper), each of which can hold a piece of data. These cells can be linked together in various ways so that a change of a piece of data in one cell immediately produces a change in all those cells to which it is connected. *The data is usually numbers, but does not have to be. The example below shows part of a spreadsheet in action.*

The top left-hand corner of a spreadsheet looks like this. Cells are identified using the letters and numbers to get A1, C2, M15, etc.

	A	B	C	D
1				
2				
3				

The data 7, 6, 4, 5, 3, 8 has been put in, and Cells D 1 to 3 hold totals of all cells to their left. A3 to C3 hold totals of cells above them.

	A	B	C	D
1	7	6	4	*17*
2	5	3	8	*16*
3	*12*	*9*	*12*	*33*

Changing the value in A1 from 7 to 18 immediately causes D1, A3, and D3 to change as they recalculate their own values.

	A	B	C	D
1	18	6	4	*28*
2	5	3	8	*16*
3	*23*	*9*	*12*	*44*

Modern spreadsheets can have over 4 million cells and hundreds of different formulas to link them. They are also capable of presenting the data in a wide variety of ways.

calculator A calculator usually refers to a small hand-held device that allows numbers to be entered, mathematical operations carried out (electronically), and the results displayed on a very small screen. For a basic model the operations are usually restricted to $+ - \times \div$ and $\sqrt{\ }$ and the display usually shows eight digits. There is sometimes a memory facility, but all data is lost when the calculator is switched off.

$$\boxed{1\,2\,3\,4\,5\,6\,7\,8}$$

scientific calculator A scientific calculator is a **calculator** that can carry out many more operations (in trigonometry, statistics, etc.). It has a slightly bigger display so that it can show large numbers in **scientific notation.**

programmable calculator A programmable calculator is a **scientific calculator** in which small programs can be keyed in, so it serves as a simple **computer**. It also has a memory which does not lose its contents when switched off.

graphics calculator A graphics calculator is a **programmable calculator** that has a larger display screen, so that graphs, text, and numbers can be shown. It has a larger memory space and no data is lost when the power is switched off. *With each new model that is brought out, more facilities are included, so that graphics calculators are becoming more powerful and more like miniature computers.*
The diagram shows the display when the line y = 3x + 5 and the parabola y = 4x² − 6 are drawn on the same axes. It also gives the coordinates of one of the intersections.

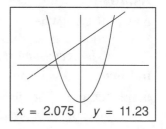

x = 2.075   y = 11.23

kinematics is the branch of mathematics dealing with the motion of objects and considering only their movement in relation to space and time, disregarding the effects of their mass or any forces acting upon them.

speed The speed of a moving object is a measure of the distance traveled by the object in a unit period of time. *Any suitable units may be used for the distance (meters, feet, miles, kilometers, etc.) and the time (hours, minutes, seconds, etc.).*

average speed When an object moves through some distance its **speed** may vary as it travels, but its average speed is found by considering only the total time taken for the move and the total distance moved. *The three equations used in working with average speed are:*

$$\text{Speed} = \text{Distance} \div \text{Time} \qquad \text{Time} = \text{Distance} \div \text{Speed}$$
$$\text{Distance} = \text{Speed} \times \text{Time}$$

Example: A car is driven from Boston to Chicago, a distance of 960 miles, and the journey takes 20 hours. What is the average speed for the journey? The average speed is 960 ÷ 20 = 48 miles per hour.

velocity The velocity of a moving object is given by stating both its **speed** and the direction in which the object is moving. *It is a **vector** quantity. If the velocity is stated without reference to any direction, it must be assumed that the object is traveling in a straight line and that the overall direction of that line does not matter. Velocity is very commonly used to mean the same as speed. The SI unit of velocity is meters per second, abbreviated to m/s or m s^{-1}.*

acceleration The acceleration of a moving object is a measure of how its **velocity** is changing in relation to time. *It is a vector quantity but its direction is often ignored and it is applied only to the speed component of the velocity. It may be positive (for speeding up) or negative (for slowing down). The SI unit of acceleration is meters per second per second, abbreviated to m/s^2 or m s^{-2}.*
Example: Starting from rest (= zero velocity) an object is given a steady acceleration of 3 m s^{-2}. What is its velocity after 10 seconds?
In this case, the object's velocity will increase by 3 m s^{-1} after every second of travel. So its velocity after 1 second is 3 m s^{-1}, after 2 seconds is 6 m s^{-1}, after 3 seconds is 9 m s^{-1}, ..., and after 10 seconds is 30 m s^{-1}.

deceleration If the **velocity** of a moving object is decreasing, then its **acceleration** is negative and is often described as deceleration.

retardation ≡ **deceleration**

constant ... When the property named in "..." does not change during the period of time being considered, that property is described as constant. *So we have constant speed, constant velocity, constant acceleration.*

uniform ... ≡ **constant ...**

displacement The displacement of an object in motion is the distance and direction from its starting position to its finishing position. It is a vector.

distance–time graph   A distance–time graph is a **graph** that shows the distance moved by an object in relation to time. *The **slope** of a line drawn on the distance–time graph is a measure of* **velocity**.

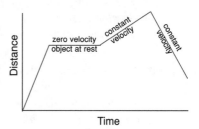

If the line of the relationship is curved, the particular velocity at some moment in time can be found only by drawing a **tangent to the curve** *at that point and measuring its slope.*

velocity–time graph   A velocity–time graph is a **graph** that shows the velocity of an object in relation to time. *The **slope** of a line drawn on the graph is a measure of* **acceleration**.

If the line of the relationship is curved, the particular acceleration at some moment in time can be found only by drawing a **tangent to the curve** *at that point and measuring its slope. The* **area under the curve** *(or the line of relationship) between two* **ordinates** *drawn from the time scale measures the distance traveled in that time interval.*

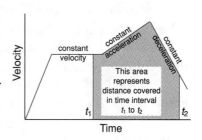

compound measures   are those measures that require more than one unit to give their value. *Units such as meters, seconds, and feet are used for single measures. One of the most commonly used compound measures is speed (in units of meters/second, miles/hour, etc.). Other examples of compound measures are density, work, power, and fuel consumption.*

To change compound units of speed from one in the left-hand column into one of those on the right, **multiply** by the number given in the table.				
To change ⌐ into →	mph	kmph	m s⁻¹	ft/second
miles per hour (mph)	1	1.6093	0.44704	1.4667
kilometers per hour (kmph)	0.62137	1	0.27778	0.91134
meters per second (m s⁻¹)	2.2369	3.6	1	3.2808
feet per second (ft/second)	0.68182	1.0973	0.3048	1

equations of uniform motion   There are five equations giving the relationships among the five variables controlling movement under conditions of uniform motion:

$$v = u + at$$
$$s = \tfrac{1}{2}(u + v)t$$
$$s = ut + \tfrac{1}{2}at^2$$
$$s = vt - \tfrac{1}{2}at^2$$
$$v^2 = u^2 + 2as$$

where

u is the initial velocity
v is the final velocity
s is the distance moved
a is the acceleration
t is the time taken

logic The logic of a system is the whole structure of rules that must be used for any reasoning within that system. *Most of mathematics is based on a well understood structure of rules and is considered to be highly logical. It is always necessary to state, or otherwise have it understood, what rules are being used before any logic can be applied.*

statement A statement made within a **logical** system is a form of words (or symbols) which carries information. *Within mathematics nearly everything is written in the form of statements.*
Examples: The length of the radius is 4 cm. $3x + 2 = 7$

argument An argument is a set of one or more **statements** which uses the **logic** of the system to show how one particular statement is arrived at.

true Within a system, a **statement** is said to be true when it is a known fact, or follows from some other true statement by means of a **valid argument**, or is considered to be **self-evident**.

false Within a system, a **statement** is said to be false when it is contrary to a statement known to be **true**.

undecidable Within a system, a **statement** is said to be undecidable when it cannot be shown to be either **true** or **false**.

assumption An assumption is a **statement** (true or false) which is to be taken as **true** for the purpose of the **argument** which follows.

premise ≡ **assumption**

self-evident A **statement** is described as self-evident when it is thought that no reasoning is necessary to demonstrate that the statement is **true**. *This is often used to describe the most basic ideas of a system which are generally "known" but are impossible to define independently of the system.*
Example: The statement "Any two things which are each equal to a third thing must be equal to each other" could be seen as being self-evident.

intuitive Understanding (of a statement or a piece of knowledge) is described as intuitive when it is, or can be, reached without support of any **argument**.

axiom An axiom is a **statement** which is assumed to be **true**, and is used as a basis for developing a system. *Any system of logic starts by saying clearly what axioms it uses.*

proposition A proposition is a **statement** whose correctness (or otherwise) is to be shown by the use of an **argument**. *It most often serves as an introduction by saying, in effect, what the argument is going to show.*

valid A valid **proof** (or **statement**) is one in which all the **arguments** leading up to it are correct within the logic of the system being used.

invalid An invalid **proof** (or **statement**) is one which is NOT **valid**.

counterexample A counterexample to a **statement** is a particular instance of where that statement is not **true**. *This makes the statement invalid.*
Only ONE counterexample is needed to make a statement invalid.
Example: "All prime numbers are odd": a counterexample is 2

proof A proof is a sequence of **statements** (made up of **axioms**, **assumptions**, and **arguments**) leading to the establishment of the **truth** of one final statement.

direct proof A direct proof is a **proof** in which all the **assumptions** used are **true** and all the **arguments** are **valid**.
Example: To prove the proposition that adding two odd numbers makes an even number. Any odd number is of the form 2n + 1
Adding two of this form produces (2n + 1) + (2m + 1)
= 2(n + m) + 2 = 2(n + m + 1), which is clearly even.

indirect proof An indirect proof is a **proof** in which one **false assumption** is made. Then, using **valid arguments**, a **statement** is arrived at which is clearly wrong; so the original assumption must have been wrong. *Indirect proofs can be used only in a system in which statements must be either true or false, so that proving the first assumption is wrong allows only one possibility for its alternative form—which must be the correct one.*
Example: To prove $\sqrt{2}$ is irrational. First assume that it is rational.

Then $\sqrt{2} = \dfrac{a}{b}$, where a, b are whole numbers with no common factors.

This leads to $a^2 = 2b^2$, and a^2 must be even and so must a.

Put $a = 2c$, then $\sqrt{2} = \dfrac{2c}{b}$ and $2c^2 = b^2$ and b must be even.

But a,b had no common factors so both cannot be even.
The assumption must be wrong and $\sqrt{2}$ is NOT rational.
$\sqrt{2}$ must be irrational.

proof by contradiction ≡ **indirect proof**

reductio ad absurdum ≡ **indirect proof**

proof by exhaustion A proof by exhaustion is a **proof** which is established by working through EVERY possible case and finding no contradictions. *Usually such a proof is possible only if the proposition to be proved has some restrictions placed upon it.*
Example: The statement "Between every pair of square numbers there is at least one prime number" would be impossible to prove by looking at every possibility. However, by writing it as "Between every pair of square numbers less than 1000 there is at least one prime number," it can be proved by exhaustion—looking at every case. This might then be considered as enough evidence to make it a **conjecture** *about all numbers.*

proof by induction A proof by induction is a **proof** which shows that IF one particular case is **true** then so is the next one; it also shows that one particular case IS true. *From those two actions it must follow that ALL cases are true.*

visual proof A visual proof is a **proof** in which the **statements** are presented in the form of diagrams.
Example: To prove the proposition that adding two odd numbers makes an even number. Any odd number can be shown as
Adding two odd numbers is shown
and clearly makes an even number.

look-see proof ≡ **visual proof**

logic (practice)

conjecture A conjecture is a **statement** which, although much evidence can be found to support it, has not been proved to be either **true** or **false**.

hypothesis A hypothesis is a **statement** which is usually thought to be true, and serves as a starting point in looking for **arguments** (or evidence) to support it. *This method is used mostly in statistics.*

theorem A theorem is a **statement** which has been **proved** to be **true**.

lemma A lemma is a **theorem** which is used in the **proof** of another theorem. *Usually a lemma is of no importance in itself, but it is a useful way of simplifying the proof of the final theorem by reducing its length.*

corollary A corollary follows after a **theorem** and is a **proposition** which must be **true** because of that theorem.
Example: It can be proved that the three interior angles of a triangle add up to 180° (a theorem). A corollary is that the exterior angle at one vertex must equal the sum of the interior angles of the other two vertices.

converse The converse of a **theorem** (or statement) is formed by taking the conclusion as the starting point and having the starting point as the conclusion. *Though any theorem can be re-formed in this way, the result may or may not be true and it needs its own proof.*
Example: One theorem states that if a triangle has two sides of equal length, then the angles opposite to those sides are also equal in size. The converse is that if a triangle has two angles of equal size, then the sides opposite to those angles must be equal in length—and that can also be proved.

contrapositive The contrapositive of a **statement** is formed by taking the conclusion as the starting point and the starting point as the conclusion and then changing the sense of each (from positive to negative and vice versa). *If the original statement was true, then the contrapositive must also be true.*
Example: The statement "If a number IS even, it CAN be divided by 2" has the contrapositive "If a number CANNOT be divided by 2, then it is NOT even."

necessary condition A necessary condition for a **statement** Q to be **true** is another statement P which MUST be true whenever statement Q is true; then statement P is said to be a necessary condition. *When P is true then Q may be true or false, but when P is false, then Q must also be false.*
Example: A necessary condition for the statement (Q) "x is divisible by 6" is statement (P) "x is even," but condition (P) by itself allows values such as 2, 4, 8, which are clearly not divisible by 6

sufficient condition A sufficient condition for a **statement** Q to be **true** is another statement P which, when P is true, guarantees that statement Q MUST also be true. *When statement P is false then statement Q may be true or false.*
Example: A sufficient condition for the statement (Q) "x is divisible by 6" is statement (P) "x is divisible by 12," but condition (P) by itself excludes values such as 6, 18, 30, which are also divisible by 6

necessary and sufficient condition A necessary and sufficient condition for a **statement** to be **true** is a second statement such that BOTH the first and the second statement MUST be true at the same time. *Both statements will be false together as well, but it cannot be that one is true and one is false.*
Example: A necessary and sufficient condition for the statement "x is divisible by 6" is that "x is even and divisible by 3"

paradox A paradox is a **valid statement** which is self-contradictory or appears to be wrong. *Paradoxes are important to the development of logic systems. Example: "The barber shaves all the men in this village who do not shave themselves" seems a reasonably clear statement. However, given that the barber is a man and lives in that village, who shaves the barber?*

fallacy A fallacy is an **argument** which seems to be correct but which contains at least one error and, as a consequence, produces a final statement which is clearly wrong. *Though it is clear that the result is wrong, the error in the argument is usually (and ought to be) difficult to find.*
Example: Let $x = y$: Then $x^2 = xy$ and $x^2 - y^2 = xy - y^2$
This gives $(x + y)(x - y) = y(x - y)$ so that dividing both sides by $(x - y)$
leaves $x + y = y$

From this result, putting $x = y = 1$ means $2 = 1$
Or, subtracting y from both sides means x (= any number) $= 0$
The error is in dividing by $(x - y)$, which is zero.

symbols The conventional way of representing statements is by using capital letters. *The letters most often used are P and Q.*
Example: P could represent "x is a prime number greater than 2"

$\mathbf{P \Rightarrow Q}$ where P and Q are statements, is a symbolic way of saying "P implies Q"; OR "when P is true then so is Q"; OR "P is a **sufficient condition** for Q." *It also means that Q is a necessary condition for P.*
Example: If P represents "x is a prime number greater than 2," and Q represents "x is an odd number," then $P \Rightarrow Q$.

$\mathbf{P \Leftarrow Q}$ where P and Q are statements, is a symbolic way of saying "P is implied by Q"; OR "when Q is true, then so also is P"; OR "P is a **necessary condition** for Q." *It also means that Q is a sufficient condition for P.*
Example: If P is "x is divisible by 5" and Q is "x is divisible by 10," then $P \Leftarrow Q$, which is a symbolic way of stating that a number which is divisible by 10 is also divisible by 5; or of saying that it is necessary (but not sufficient) that a number is divisible by 5 if it is to be divisible by 10

$\mathbf{P \Leftrightarrow Q}$ where P and Q are statements, is a symbolic way of saying that P and Q must both be true (or false) together; OR "P implies and is implied by Q"; OR "P is a **necessary and sufficient condition** for Q."
Example: If P is "x is divisible by 6" and Q is "x is divisible by 2 and 3," then $P \Rightarrow Q$ and $P \Rightarrow Q$ so $P \Leftrightarrow Q$.

iff is a short way of writing "if and only if" and is equivalent to $\Leftrightarrow$.
Example: In the previous example the final statement could be "P iff Q."

array An array is an orderly display of data arranged in a rectangular shape.

element An element of an **array** is one complete piece of the data in the array.

Example: In the array $\begin{array}{cc} 3.8 & 4.2 \\ 6.1 & 7.9 \end{array}$ *3.8 is an element, but 8 is not, since it is not the complete piece of data.*

matrix A matrix is a rectangular **array** of **elements**. *Usually the elements are all of the same type (numbers, symbols, algebraic expressions, etc.) and the array is enclosed in either square or round brackets. The individual elements are separated only by spaces; commas or other dividing marks are not used.*

Example: $\begin{pmatrix} 1 & 4 & ^-3 \\ 6 & 1.5 & 7 \end{pmatrix}$ $\begin{pmatrix} A & X \\ Y & B \end{pmatrix}$ $\begin{pmatrix} 3x+8 & y+1 \\ 3y-4 & 2x-7 \end{pmatrix}$

row A row of a **matrix** is the set of **elements** making up one complete line reading across the matrix from left to right.

Example: *The matrix* $\begin{pmatrix} 1 & 7 \\ 8 & 5 \end{pmatrix}$ *has 2 rows: 1   7 and 8   5*

column A column of a **matrix** is the set of **elements** making up one complete line reading down the matrix from top to bottom.

Example: *The matrix* $\begin{pmatrix} 4 & 9 & 6 \\ 1 & 0 & 7 \end{pmatrix}$ *has 3 columns.*

order The order of a **matrix** is a measure of its size, giving it as "the number of **rows** by the number of **columns**" it has. *They must be stated that way round.*

Example: $\begin{pmatrix} 7 & ^-6 & 0 & 3 \\ 9 & 1 & 8 & 3 \end{pmatrix}$ *is a 2 by 4 matrix.*

square matrix A square matrix has the same number of **rows** and **columns**.

Example: $\begin{pmatrix} 4 & ^-1 \\ 0 & 6 \end{pmatrix}$ *is a square matrix. It is also a 2-by-2 matrix.*

row matrix A row matrix has only a single **row**.

Example: (3   ^-4   10)   is a row matrix. It is also a 1-by-3 matrix.

column matrix A column matrix has only a single **column**.

diagonals The set of **elements** making up one complete line reading from the top left corner to the bottom right corner of a **square matrix** is the **leading, main,** or **principal diagonal**. *The other line (from top right to bottom left) is the* **secondary** *or* **trailing diagonal**.

Example: In $\begin{pmatrix} 7 & 2 \\ 4 & ^-9 \end{pmatrix}$ *the main diagonal is   7   ^-9 and the trailing diagonal is   2   4*

trace The trace of a **square matrix** is the sum of the elements in the **main diagonal**

Example: In $\begin{pmatrix} ^-6 & 10 \\ 14 & 18 \end{pmatrix}$ *the trace is 12 (= ^-6 + 18)*

transpose The transpose of a **matrix** is made by rewriting the **rows** of the matrix as **columns**. *In a square matrix the leading diagonal will be unchanged.*

Example: For $\begin{pmatrix} a & b & c \\ d & e & f \end{pmatrix}$ *the transpose is* $\begin{pmatrix} a & d \\ b & e \\ c & f \end{pmatrix}$

addition Two matrices may be added, provided that they are of the same **order**, by adding corresponding elements in each to form a new element for the solution matrix. *The solution matrix will also be of the same order.*

Example: $\begin{pmatrix} 1 & 2 \\ 3 & 4 \end{pmatrix} + \begin{pmatrix} 5 & 9 \\ 7 & 8 \end{pmatrix} \rightarrow \begin{pmatrix} 1+5 & 2+9 \\ 3+7 & 4+8 \end{pmatrix} = \begin{pmatrix} 6 & 11 \\ 10 & 12 \end{pmatrix}$

scalar multiplication A scalar is a number which, when written in front (to the left) of a **matrix**, means that all the **elements** of that matrix have to be multiplied by that number.

Example: $\mathbf{3} \begin{pmatrix} 2 & 0 \\ 1 & 5 \end{pmatrix} \rightarrow \begin{pmatrix} \mathbf{3} \times 2 & \mathbf{3} \times 0 \\ \mathbf{3} \times 1 & \mathbf{3} \times 5 \end{pmatrix} = \begin{pmatrix} 6 & 0 \\ 3 & 15 \end{pmatrix}$

multiplication Two matrices may be multiplied, provided that the number of COLUMNS in the FIRST matrix is the same as the number of ROWS in the SECOND matrix. *It is done by laying each row of the first matrix against each column of the second matrix, multiplying the pairs of elements, and adding the results together to make a single element for the answer matrix. Matrix multiplication depends on the ORDER in which the two are written. Changing the order may give a different answer, or multiplication may not be possible. Example:*

$\begin{pmatrix} 4 & 2 \\ 3 & 1 \end{pmatrix}\begin{pmatrix} 5 & 7 & 8 \\ 6 & 0 & 9 \end{pmatrix} \rightarrow \begin{pmatrix} 4 \times 5 + 2 \times 6 & 4 \times 7 + 2 \times 0 & 4 \times 8 + 2 \times 9 \\ 3 \times 5 + 1 \times 6 & 3 \times 7 + 1 \times 0 & 3 \times 8 + 1 \times 9 \end{pmatrix} = \begin{pmatrix} 32 & 28 & 50 \\ 21 & 21 & 33 \end{pmatrix}$

But $\begin{pmatrix} 5 & 7 & 8 \\ 6 & 0 & 9 \end{pmatrix} \begin{pmatrix} 4 & 2 \\ 3 & 1 \end{pmatrix}$ *cannot be done.*

diagonal matrix A diagonal matrix is a **square matrix** which has all its **elements** equal to zero, except for those on the **main diagonal**.

identity matrix The identity matrix (for multiplication) is a **square matrix** whose **elements** in the **main diagonal** are all 1's, and the others are all zero.

Example: $\begin{pmatrix} 1 & 0 \\ 0 & 1 \end{pmatrix}$ *is the 2-by-2 identity matrix (for multiplication).*

determinant The determinant of a **square matrix** is a single number obtained by applying a particular set of rules to the **elements** of that matrix.

$\begin{vmatrix} a & b \\ c & d \end{vmatrix}$ The two ruled lines are a symbol meaning that the **determinant** of the matrix $\begin{pmatrix} a & b \\ c & d \end{pmatrix}$ has to be found.

For a 2-by-2 matrix the rule is $ad - bc$

Example: $\begin{vmatrix} 2 & 3 \\ 4 & 7 \end{vmatrix}$ *is* $(2 \times 7) - (3 \times 4) = 14 - 12 = 2$

singular matrix A singular matrix is a **square matrix** with **determinant** = zero.

inverse matrix The inverse, for multiplication, of a **square matrix** (which must NOT be **singular**) is another matrix such that when the two are multiplied together, in any order, the result is the **identity matrix**. *Example:*

The inverse of $\begin{pmatrix} 2 & 1 \\ 5 & 3 \end{pmatrix}$ *is* $\begin{pmatrix} 3 & ^{-}1 \\ ^{-}5 & 2 \end{pmatrix}$ *since* $\begin{pmatrix} 2 & 1 \\ 5 & 3 \end{pmatrix} \begin{pmatrix} 3 & ^{-}1 \\ ^{-}5 & 2 \end{pmatrix} = \begin{pmatrix} 1 & 0 \\ 0 & 1 \end{pmatrix}$

direction For movement over the surface of the earth, the direction (of a line) is measured relative to another line pointing to a position called north. *There are two positions known as north. The North Pole is fixed and known as true north. A magnetic compass points at magnetic north. The difference between true north and magnetic north varies and can be as much as 20°.*

points of the compass The points of the compass are those directions defined (relative to north) by dividing a circle into 4, 8, 16, or 32 equal parts. *The principal points are north, south, east, and west, and the next four are the points between those: northeast (NE), etc.*

compass angles are the angles (in degrees) measured CLOCKWISE from the north line to the line of the required direction. *This allows a direction to be given to any (possible) accuracy between 0° and 360°. Such angles are always written with 3 digits, so 57° becomes 057° and 6° is 006°.*

bearing The bearing of position B FROM position A is the **direction** (usually given as a **compass angle**) in which someone traveling in a straight line FROM A TO B must go. *Care should be taken when using "from" and "to" in this work.*

reciprocal bearing A reciprocal bearing is the direction which is the reverse of the given **bearing**. *If the given bearing is FROM A TO B, the reciprocal bearing is the bearing FROM B TO A.*
> If bearing is LESS than 180°, ADD 180° to get the reciprocal.
> If bearing is MORE than 180°, SUBTRACT 180° to get the reciprocal.

back bearing ≡ **reciprocal bearing**

pole A pole is one of two positions (one north, one south) on the earth's surface through which the **axis of rotation** of the earth passes.

great circle A great circle is any circle drawn on the surface of a sphere (the earth) whose center is at the center of the sphere. *All great circles on a sphere are of the same size, and any one divides the sphere into two hemispheres.*

small circle A small circle is any circle drawn on the surface of a sphere (the earth) that is NOT a **great circle**.

equator The equator is the **great circle** around the earth that is perpendicular to the **axis of rotation**. *It is equidistant from either pole, and divides the earth into northern and southern hemispheres.*

latitude A line of latitude is a **small circle** on the earth's surface, parallel to the **equator**, whose position is given north or south of the equator.

meridian A meridian is half of a **great circle** on the earth's surface going from one **pole** to the other. *It appears as a line running north and south, crossing the equator at right angles.*

Greenwich Meridian The Greenwich Meridian is the **meridian** which passes through a fixed point in the old Greenwich Observatory (in London).

longitude A line of longitude is a **meridian** whose position is given, east or west, relative to the **Greenwich Meridian** as measured by the angle at the center of the earth between the **great circles** forming those two meridians.

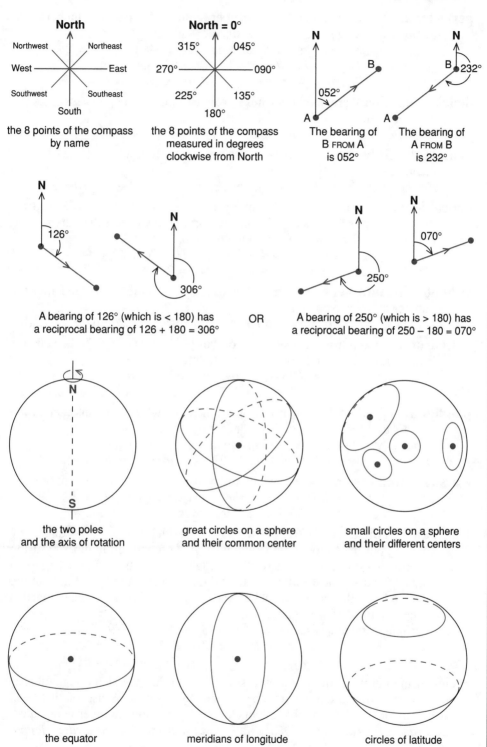

North

Northwest — Northeast
West — East
Southwest — Southeast
South

the 8 points of the compass
by name

North = 0°

315°   045°
270° — 090°
225°   135°
180°

the 8 points of the compass
measured in degrees
clockwise from North

N

B
052°
A

The bearing of
B FROM A
is 052°

N

B 232°
A

The bearing of
A FROM B
is 232°

N
126°

N
306°

A bearing of 126° (which is < 180) has
a reciprocal bearing of 126 + 180 = 306°

OR

N

250°

N
070°

A bearing of 250° (which is > 180) has
a reciprocal bearing of 250 − 180 = 070°

N

S

the two poles
and the axis of rotation

great circles on a sphere
and their common center

small circles on a sphere
and their different centers

the equator

meridians of longitude

circles of latitude

perfect numbers are numbers whose **proper factors** add up to the number itself.
 Examples: 6 is a perfect number, since 1 + 2 + 3 = 6
 28 is a perfect number, since 1 + 2 + 4 + 7 + 14 = 28
 The next three are 496, 8128, and 33,550,336
 No odd perfect numbers are known.

deficient numbers are numbers whose **proper factors** add up to LESS THAN the number itself.
 Example: 16 is a deficient number, since 1 + 2 + 4 + 8 = 15

abundant numbers are numbers whose **proper factors** add up to MORE THAN the number itself.
 Example: 20 is an abundant number, since 1 + 2 + 4 + 5 + 10 = 22

amicable pair An amicable pair of numbers is two numbers with the property that the **proper factors** of each one add up to the value of the other.
 Example: 220 and 284 are an amicable pair.
 220 gives 1 + 2 + 4 + 5 + 10 + 11 + 20 + 22 + 44 + 55 = 284
 284 gives 1 + 2 + 4 + 71 + 142 = 220

automorphic numbers are numbers whose last digits are unchanged after the number has been squared.
 Example: 76 and 625 are automorphic, since $76^2 = 5776$; $625^2 = 390,625$

palindrome A palindrome is a number (or word) which is unchanged whether it is read from left to right or from right to left.
 Examples: 77 565 34,843 1,962,691 are all palindromic numbers.
 11 727 36,563 9,714,179 are all palindromic primes.

pandigital A pandigital number or expression is one which contains each of the digits 1 to 9 (or 0 to 9) once and once only.
 Examples: 26 + 48 + 79 = 153 is a pandigital expression.
 139,854,276 and 9,814,072,356 are pandigital squares.

Harshad numbers are numbers which can be divided exactly by their **digit sum**.
 Example: 1729 is a Harshad number, since its digit sum (1 + 7 + 2 + 9)
 is 19, and 19 divides exactly into 1729

Kaprekar's constant = 6174. This is the result eventually produced by carrying out the following operations. Make a four-digit number by using at least two different, nonzero digits. Place the digits in order: largest to smallest and smallest to largest, to make two other numbers. Subtract the smaller from the larger to make a new number. Continue repeating this process until 6174 is obtained.
 Example: Starting with 1998:   1998 → 9981 − 1899 = 8082
 8082 → 8820 − 0288 = 8532
 *8532 → 8532 − 2358 = **6174***

cycles using numbers are found by first making a rule by which one number is used to produce another number. Then, by continuous use of that rule, determine if a loop or chain is made when a previous number is repeated.
 *By using the rule given to make **happy numbers** some cycles will be found.*

partition To partition a number is to break it up into a separate set of numbers which add up to make the original number. *Whole numbers are used throughout. Zero is not used but the number itself is included. Merely reordering the set is not considered to represent a different partition. The number of different ways in which each of the numbers 1 to 10 may be partitioned are shown in the table on the right.*
Example: 5 can be partitioned in 7 different ways as:

Number	Ways
1	1
2	2
3	3
4	5
5	7
6	11
7	15
8	22
9	30
10	42

1 + 1 + 1 + 1 + 1   1 + 1 + 1 + 2   1 + 1 + 3
1 + 2 + 2   1 + 4   2 + 3   5

persistence The digits of a number are multiplied together to make another number. This process is continued on each new number until only a single digit is obtained. The number of times the process has to be repeated to achieve this is a measure of the persistence of the original number.
Example: $79 \rightarrow 63 \rightarrow 18 \rightarrow 8$ so 79 has a persistence of 3

polite numbers have been defined as those numbers which can be made by adding together two or more consecutive whole numbers. *This can often be done in more than one way, and the number of ways it can be done is a measure of the politeness of a number.*
Example: $15 = 1 + 2 + 3 + 4 + 5$ and $4 + 5 + 6$ and $7 + 8$, so 15 is
a polite number and has a politeness of 3

happy numbers A number has all its digits squared and added together to make a new number. This process is repeated until a 1 is obtained, at which point the original number is described as happy. *If a 1 is never obtained, the original number is said to be sad.*
Example: $19 \rightarrow 1^2 + 9^2 = 82 \rightarrow 8^2 + 2^2 = 68 \rightarrow 6^2 + 8^2 = 100 \rightarrow 1^2 = 1$
so 19 is a happy number.

cutting numbers have been defined as that sequence of numbers produced when a given shape is cut up into the maximum number of pieces by a succession of 1, 2, 3, 4 . . . cuts and without rearranging the pieces between cuts.
Examples: A line makes 2, 3, 4, 5 . . . pieces after 1, 2, 3, 4 . . . cuts.
A circle produces 2, 4, 7, 11 . . . pieces after 1, 2, 3, 4 . . . cuts.

repunits are numbers made up only of 1's (= *repeated units*). *A short way of writing such numbers is I_n where n is the number of 1's to be used.*
Examples: $I_3 = 111$ $I_6 = 111,111$ I_2 I_{19} I_{23} are all primes.

multigrades A multigrade is an equality between two expressions, each requiring some numbers to be raised to a power and added, which is true for more than one value of that power.
Examples: $1^n + 2^n + 6^n = 4^n + 5^n$ (n = 1 or 2)
$1^n + 6^n + 8^n = 2^n + 4^n + 9^n$ (n = 1 or 2)

digital invariants are those numbers which are equal to the sum of all their separate digits when raised to the same power.
Example: 153 is a digital invariant, since $1^3 + 5^3 + 3^3 = 1 + 125 + 27 = 153$

superscript A superscript is a letter or number written in small type placed to the right and at the top of a letter, number, or symbol written full size.
  Example: In A^2 A^n 5^2 7^x y^3 ^{2} ^{n} ^{2} ^{x} *and* ^{3} *are all superscripts.*

subscript A subscript is a letter or number written in small type placed to the right and at the bottom of a letter, number, or symbol written in full size.
  Example: In A_1 A_3 B_n x_2 x_r $_1$ $_3$ $_n$ $_2$ *and* $_r$ *are all subscripts.*

exponent notation is a way of indicating how a number (or symbol) must be operated on by using another number written as a **superscript** to the first; this second number is called an exponent. *When the exponent is a positive whole number, that number indicates how many of the first number or symbol must be multiplied together. When the exponent is a fraction, it indicates that a root has to be found.*
  Examples: $A^2 = A \times A$ $5^3 = 5 \times 5 \times 5 = 125$ $9^{\frac{1}{2}} = \sqrt{9} = 3$

base In **exponent notation** the base is the number (or symbol) upon which the **exponent** is to operate.
  Examples: In A^2 y^{-1} 3^4 10^x *A, y, 3, and 10 are all bases.*

positive exponent A positive exponent is an **exponent** which is greater than zero.

zero exponent A zero exponent is an **exponent** which is equal to zero. *ANY number (except zero) raised to a zero exponent is equal to 1.*
  Example: $1^0 = 1$; $2^0 = 1$; $5^0 = 1$;   *(any number)*$^0 = 1$; $x^0 = 1$

negative exponent An **exponent** having a negative value indicates that a **reciprocal** has to be taken BEFORE the exponent is applied to the **base**.
  Examples: $x^{-1} = \dfrac{1}{x}$ $x^{-2} = \dfrac{1}{x^2}$ $2^{-3} = \dfrac{1}{2^3} = \dfrac{1}{8}$

power ≡ **exponent**

index The index of a **root** is a number showing the degree of the root.

scientific notation is a way of displaying a number in the form of a first number, whose value lies between 1 and 10, and a second number which is always 10 with a suitable **exponent**, so that the two numbers multiplied together equal the value of the intended number.
  Examples: 1.436×10^2 *means 143.6* $1.436 \times 10^{-3} = 0.001436$

Scientific notation is shown differently on electronic calculators, where 1.436 × 10^2 would appear as 1.436E02

reciprocal The reciprocal of a number is the value given by dividing 1 BY that number, or dividing that number INTO 1
  Examples: The reciprocal of 2 is $\dfrac{1}{2}$ *or* $1 \div 2 = 0.5$

  of 7 is $\dfrac{1}{7} = 0.142857\ldots$

factorial   The value of factorial n is found by multiplying together all the whole numbers from 1 up to, and including, n. A special case is $0! = 1$
Example: Factorial 5 is $5 \times 4 \times 3 \times 2 \times 1 = 120$

!   when written AFTER the number n is the symbol for **factorial** n. *Example: $5! = 120$*

0!	=	1
1!	=	1
2!	=	2
3!	=	6
4!	=	24
5!	=	120
6!	=	720
7!	=	5040
8!	=	40,320
9!	=	362,880
10!	=	3,628,800

permutation   A permutation of a set of objects is an ORDERED arrangement of those objects. *The fact that it is ordered means that* AB *is considered to be different from* BA. *Interest is usually focused on how many different permutations are possible from a given set of objects.*
Example: Set ABC *has 6 permutations:* ABC, ACB, BAC, BCA, CAB, CBA
With n different objects there are $n!$ permutations possible.

$_n\mathbf{P}_r$ is the symbol for the total number of **permutations** possible when, from a set of n objects, r are chosen at a time.
When the objects are all distinguishably different, then $_n\mathbf{P}_r = \dfrac{n!}{(n-r)!}$

combination   A combination of objects is an UNORDERED arrangement of those objects. *The fact that it is unordered means that* ABC *is considered to be the same as* BCA *or* CAB *or* CBA, *etc.*

$_n\mathbf{C}_r$ is the symbol for the total number of **combinations** possible when, from a set of n objects, r are chosen at a time. *Said as "From n choose r"*
When the objects are all distinguishably different, then $_n\mathbf{C}_r = \dfrac{n!}{(n-r)!\,r!}$
When $r = n$ then $_n\mathbf{C}_r = 1$
Example: $_{49}\mathbf{C}_6 = \dfrac{49!}{43! \times 6!} = 13,983,816$ (which is almost 14 million)

logarithms   The logarithm as an aid to computation was invented by John Napier, a Scottish mathematician, in the sixteenth century. It depends on the fact that when two numbers with the same base are multiplied or divided, the base is kept and the exponents are added or subtracted.
Examples: $2^3 \times 2^5 = 2^8$ $x^7 \div x^4 = x^3$

Since addition and subtraction are usually easier than multiplication and division, if the statements are written in **logarithmic form** *the computation is made easier. In practice, the base usually used is 10 and the actual logarithms are found in a table or from a calculator.*

logarithmic vs. exponential form   A number in exponential form can be written in logarithmic form as follows:
exponential form: $2^3 = 8$ logarithmic form: $\log_2 8 = 3$

common logarithms   are the most commonly used logarithms. They use a base of 10.

natural logarithms   are used in calculus and some scientific work. They use a base of e ($e \approx 2.718$).

Naperian logarithms $\equiv$ **natural logarithms**

number system A number system is made up of a set of defined symbols and the numbers they represent, together with rules for forming larger numbers from those symbols.

Hindu–Arabic number system The Hindu–Arabic number system is the **number system** which is used for ordinary **arithmetic**; and the symbols are the **digits** 0 to 9

place value A place value **number system** is one in which the positions of the symbols affect the overall value of the number. *Early number systems did not use a place value system, and it is sometimes difficult to decide what the value of the number is meant to be.*
Example: In the number 7361 the symbol 3 has a value of 3 hundreds, but in the number 4138 it has a value of 3 tens.

base The base of a **place value number system** controls the relationship between the places. *Usually it is also the number of different symbols used. Example: In ordinary arithmetic the base is 10, and there are 10 symbols used to make numbers. They are 0, 1, 2, 3, 4, 5, 6, 7, 8, and 9.*

binary A binary **number system** uses a **base** of 2. *The 2 symbols used are 0 and 1. Numbers in this base look like 1001101 ($\equiv$ 77 in decimal).*

ternary A ternary **number system** uses a **base** of 3. *The 3 symbols used are 0, 1, and 2. Numbers in this base look like 1020211 ($\equiv$ 913 in decimal).*

octal An octal **number system** uses a **base** of 8. *The 8 symbols used are 0, 1, 2, 3, 4, 5, 6, and 7. This system is used in some computer work.*

decimal A decimal **number system** uses a **base** of 10. *This is the system used in ordinary arithmetic. A duodecimal system uses a base of 12.*

denary $\equiv$ **decimal**

hexadecimal A hexadecimal **number system** uses a **base** of 16. *The 16 symbols used are 0, 1, 2, 3, 4, 5, 6, 7, 8, 9, A, B, C, D, E, and F. This system is used widely in computer work. To signal that a hexadecimal number is intended it is sometimes prefaced with the symbol &. A signal is necessary because, for instance, the hexadecimal value of 10 is decimal 16. The base is usually written as a subscript.*
Example: The largest two-symbol number in the hexadecimal system is FF_{16} which is equivalent to 255 in the decimal system.

place value headings The column headings needed for any **place value system** are fixed by the **base** used in that system. The way in which this is done is shown, where b is the value of the base. *Values for the most common bases are given. The table can be extended to the right to form fractions in any system, especially decimal. The values are then b^{-1}, b^{-2}, b^{-3}, etc. giving rise to one-tenth, one-hundredth, etc. for decimals.*

		b^3	b^2	b	units
binary system	$b = 2$	8	4	2	1
ternary system	$b = 3$	81	9	3	1
octal system	$b = 8$	512	64	8	1
decimal system	$b = 10$	1000	100	10	1
duodecimal	$b = 12$	1728	144	12	1
hexadecimal	$b = 16$	4096	256	16	1

place value names are those used in the decimal system to name the columns as shown below. *Only in the decimal system are the columns named. Note how hundreds, tens, and units (h t u) are repeated under each major name.*

trillions			billions			millions			thousands			hundreds	tens	units
h	t	u	h	t	u	h	t	u	h	t	u			

place holder or **zero** The place holder in the **Hindu–Arabic number system** is the symbol for zero ($\equiv 0$). *It is necessary to have such a symbol in a place value system or else it would be impossible to know in which column each of the other symbols should be placed, and so know its true value.*
Example: In 3024 the 3 symbol is valued at 3 thousands. If the 0 was left out as there were no hundreds, then 342 would value the 3 symbol at 3 hundreds.

additive number systems are **number systems** in which the bigger numbers are formed by using enough of the basic symbols to add up to the number required. *With such systems the symbols can be placed in any order; it is necessary only to make clear to which group, or number, each symbol belongs.*

Egyptian number system Ancient Egyptians used an **additive number system**, with the symbols

$| \equiv 1 \qquad \cap \equiv 10 \qquad 9 \equiv 100 \qquad \equiv 1000 \qquad \equiv 10,000$

Example:

$\equiv 5 + 30 + 200 + 1000 = 1235$

early Roman number system The Romans mainly used an **additive number system**, with the symbols

$I \equiv 1 \quad V \equiv 5 \quad X \equiv 10 \quad L \equiv 50 \quad C \equiv 100 \quad D \equiv 500 \quad M \equiv 1000$
Examples: IIII $\equiv 4$ XXXX $\equiv 40$ LXXXX $\equiv 90$ CCCXX $\equiv 320$

later Roman number system Sometimes, to save space, the Romans used a subtractive idea in their number system: symbols now HAD to be written in size order from left to right but, if a smaller one preceded a larger one then the smaller had to be subtracted from the larger; this could be applied only to an adjacent pair of symbols. *The idea was little used by the Romans and was applied to every number only in comparatively recent times.*
Examples: IV (is 1,5 so 5 – 1) $\equiv 4$ VC (is 5,100 so 100 – 5) $\equiv 95$
IX $\equiv 9$ XLIV $\equiv 44$ MCMXLIV $\equiv 1944$ MCMXCV $\equiv 1995$

Greek number system Ancient Greeks used an **additive number system**, with their alphabet as number symbols.
Example: $\sigma \pi \theta$ (is 200 + 80 + 9) $\equiv 289$

Babylonian number system The Babylonians used a mixture of an **additive number system**, with some subtraction, and a **place value system** with a **base** of 60. *This base lingers on in our measurement of time and angle (60 minutes in 1 hour, etc.). The Babylonians needed only three symbols: for 1, 10, and subtraction. They did not have a place holder.*

natural numbers are the set of numbers 1, 2, 3, 4, 5, 6, . . . as used in counting.

counting numbers ≡ **natural numbers**

integers are numbers made from the **natural numbers** (including 0) by putting a positive or a negative sign in front. *The positive sign is often omitted.*
Examples: . . . , ⁻5, ⁻4, ⁻3, ⁻2, ⁻1, 0, 1, 2, 3, 4, 5, . . .

whole numbers are the set of natural numbers and zero.

positive integers ≡ **natural numbers**

signed numbers ≡ **integers**

directed numbers ≡ **integers**

rational numbers can be written in the form $\frac{a}{b}$ where a and b are both **integers** and b is not zero.

Examples: ⁻4.5 $1\frac{1}{3}$ $0.09090909\overline{09}$ $3.14285\overline{7}$ 8

are all rational since they can be re-written as:

$$\frac{⁻9}{2} \qquad \frac{4}{3} \qquad \frac{1}{11} \qquad \frac{22}{7} \qquad \frac{8}{1}$$

irrational numbers can be written only in number form (using no symbols) as never-ending, nonrepeating decimal fractions. *An irrational number CANNOT be written in the form of a rational number.*

Example: 1.234567891011121314151617181920212223 24...

To generate this number it is necessary only to write out the natural numbers, and it could go on forever without repeating. It is an irrational number. The square root of any prime number is irrational, as also is π.

real numbers The set of real numbers is made up of all the **rational** and **irrational** numbers together.

positive numbers are all the **real numbers** which are greater than 0.

negative numbers are all the **real numbers** which are less than 0.

$\mathbb{N}$ is the symbol to indicate that the set of **natural numbers** is to be used.

$\mathbb{Z}$ is the symbol to indicate that the set of **integers** is to be used.

$\mathbb{Q}$ is the symbol to indicate that the set of **rational numbers** is to be used.

$\mathbb{R}$ is the symbol to indicate that the set of **real numbers** is to be used.

$\mathbb{C}$ is the symbol to indicate that the set of **complex numbers** is to be used.

number line A number line is a graduated straight line along which it is possible *(in theory)* to mark ALL the **real numbers**.

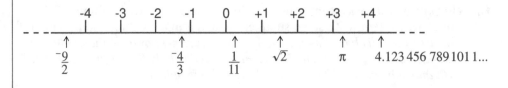

cardinal numbers are the **natural numbers** used to describe "how many" objects there are in a set.
Example: "The set R B Z N F B R X *has 8 letters all together but only 6 are different." In that statement 8 and 6 are used as cardinal numbers.*

ordinal numbers are the **natural numbers** used to describe the "position" of an object in a set which is arranged in order. *Most common are 1st, 2nd, 3rd etc.*
Example: "The set C N B I Z K F R G *has* R *as the eighth letter and in position 6 there is a* K." *In that statement 8 and 6 are used as ordinal numbers.*

identification numbers are numbers which are neither **cardinal** nor **ordinal** but which are given to objects or persons to help distinguish them in some way. *They may be part cardinal and/or part ordinal when they are made, but that usually has nothing to do with their use.*
Examples: a number 9 bus; social security numbers; a personal identification number (PIN); catalog numbers

i is the symbol for $\sqrt{^-1}$ (the square root of negative one) which cannot exist as a **real number**. **j** is also used, especially in science and engineering.

imaginary numbers are the square roots of negative numbers. *They are called imaginary because the square root of a negative number cannot be* **real**. *The way in which they are expressed is based on this argument:*
$\sqrt{^-k}$ *can always be rewritten as* $\sqrt{k} \times \sqrt{^-1}$ *and* **k** *is positive so* $\sqrt{k}$ *is real.*

Suppose $\sqrt{k} = b$; *then* $\sqrt{^-k} = \sqrt{k} \times \sqrt{^-1} = bi$
So any imaginary number can be written in the form **bi**, *where* **b** *is real.*

complex numbers involve a combination of **real** and **imaginary numbers**. *They are written in the form* **a + bi**, *where* **a** *and* **b** *are real numbers.*

Argand diagram An Argand diagram allows **complex numbers** to be shown in a way that is not possible on a simple real **number line**. *The diagram uses a number line as one axis to plot the real part of the complex number, and a second number line to form an axis at right angles to the first, on which the imaginary part of the same complex number can be plotted. With these two points as a coordinate pair, a single point can be plotted to represent the complex number. Operations on complex numbers can also be shown.*
Example showing the complex number 4 + 3i on an Argand diagram:

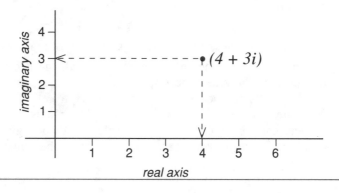

pi (π)

π (a Greek letter spelled out as **pi**) is the symbol used to represent a particular number. It is an **irrational number** and the first 50 decimal places of its value are:

3.141 592 653 589 793 238 462 643 383 279 502 884 197 169 399 375 10 . . .
For the first 5000 places see the inside covers.

π relates the radius or diameter of a **circle** to its area and to its circumference.

π has a very long history, but it was not until 1706 that the English mathematician William Jones gave it the symbol and name that we use today. However, not much notice was taken of his idea until it was published by the more famous Swiss mathematician Leonhard Euler in 1737.

The Ancient Egyptians (c.2000 BC) knew of the diameter–area relationship of a circle. They recorded that the area of a circle was found by taking eight-ninths of the diameter and squaring it. This implies a value of about 3.16 for π. The Babylonians, at about the same period, had a stated value of 3.125, which they used for their work on the circle.

Approximations for π (or its equivalent) that have been suggested at times are:

3 (*Bible: I Kings 7.23*) $\dfrac{22}{7}$ (*about 60 AD*) $3\dfrac{17}{120}$ (*150 AD*)

3.1416 (*380 AD*) $\sqrt{10}$ (*600 AD*) $\dfrac{355}{113}$ $\dfrac{333}{106}$ $\sqrt{\sqrt{\dfrac{2143}{22}}}$

All of the dated estimates were produced by careful measuring and observation.

Archimedes (c.287–212 BC), a Sicilian-Greek mathematician, was the first to work on the problem of finding the value of π in a systematic and analytical manner. He did it by "squeezing" the circle between two similar polygons, one fitting tightly inside the circle and the other outside, and considering their areas. The simplest case is for squares:

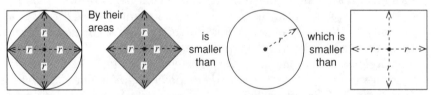

In modern terms: $2r^2 < \pi r^2 < 4r^2$ so $2 < \pi < 4$ (with a reasonable first guess for π of about 3). Archimedes started with a pair of hexagons and worked up to a pair of polygons having 96 edges. This allowed him to state that

$$3\tfrac{10}{71} < \pi < 3\tfrac{1}{7}$$

which was, for those times, a remarkable feat of mathematics.

The polygon method was the only method for calculating π for many years. Only developments in arithmetic (especially the decimal system) allowed greater accuracy to be obtained with easier working. By 1630 it had been worked out to 39 decimal places, though this was obviously far in excess of anything needed for practical work. Such an "accurate" value for π would give the circumference of the known universe to an accuracy of less than the diameter of an atom.

The seventeenth century saw the beginnings of a whole new era of mathematics. Many great mathematicians lived at this time and generated much of the mathematics that we use today. One, among many, of the new ideas was that of a **series** and, in particular, the one found by the Scottish mathematician John Gregory in 1671. It was:

$$\tan^{-1} x = x - \frac{x^3}{3} + \frac{x^5}{5} - \frac{x^7}{7} + \frac{x^9}{9} - \dots \quad (x \text{ is in radians})$$

which, provided x is less than 1 (and the smaller the better), will be accurate to several decimal places after a comparatively small number of terms. It can be used in conjunction with this formula to evaluate π:

$$\pi = 16 \tan^{-1}\left(\tfrac{1}{5}\right) - 4 \tan^{-1}\left(\tfrac{1}{239}\right)$$

The Gregory series, together with that formula and others like it, was used thereafter to calculate π. The method was used by William Shanks, who, after many years of calculating, finally published (in 1873) a value to 707 decimal places. That stood as the record until (in 1945) errors were found starting at the 528th place. These were corrected and the value then extended to 808 places. It was the last big calculation of π to be done "by hand."

In 1949 the first of the computer calculations of π was published, to 2037 places. It took 70 hours to compute using the same method as Shanks's. By 1967 it took only 28 hours to produce half a million digits using a faster series. And it didn't stop there. In 1996 a Japanese mathematician generated over 6 billion digits of π. It took 5 days.

A new algorithm for computing π has been devised in recent years and is shown on the right. It starts with the values

$A = 1, B = 0.5, C = \sqrt{2} \div 2, D = 0.25$

It is very fast and gives a value for π accurate to 170 digits in only 6 loops, and to 1 million digits in 20 loops. Its big disadvantage is that, unlike the series method described above, all the accuracy needed must be worked with from the start, which makes impossible demands on the arithmetic processes of ordinary computers without special programs.

Start

Let $E = A$

Let $B = 2 \times B$

Let $A = (A + C) \div 2$

Let $C = \sqrt{C \times E}$

Let $D = D - [B \times (A - E)^2]$

Then $\pi = (A + C)^2 \div (4 \times D)$

Loop

Why? Why do they do it? Originally because it was there to be done, but there is now much more to it than that. Computing π is a good standard exercise for checking the working of a computer. It presents an interesting challenge for those who have to write programs for computers. It provides a reason for the development of yet more mathematics. And there is always the quest to find some sort of "pattern" in what looks to be a random set of digits. That quest has not ended, but neither has it yet produced anything of great significance.

polygon numbers A polygon number is a number which, after it has been used to count a set of objects, then those objects can be arranged in the shape of a **regular polygon**. These polygons are made, starting with 1, so that each new polygon is built around the previous one in the way shown opposite. *The number is named after the shape, and a sequence can be formed of all the numbers which make that shape.*

figurate numbers ≡ **polygon numbers**

triangle numbers are **polygon numbers** having three sides.
The sequence begins 1, 3, 6, 10, 15, 21, 28, . . .
The nth triangle number is given by $n(n + 1) \div 2$

square numbers are those numbers that can be represented by the correct amount of dots laid out in rows and columns to make a square. *Some square numbers are*

   1 •   *4* • •   *9* • • •   *16* • • • •

$P_e(n)$ is used here to indicate a polygon number. It makes a polygon having e sides and that gives the number its name (3 = triangle, 4 = square, etc.). n is the number of objects along the length of one side, and is also the position of the number in the sequence.

					$n =$				
	name	1	2	3	4	5	6	7	8
$e = 3$	triangle	1	3	6	10	15	21	28	36
4	square	1	4	9	16	25	36	49	64
5	pentagon	1	5	12	22	35	51	70	92

Some values of $P_e(n)$ for various values of n and e

The general formula is $P_e(n) = n [2 + (e - 2) (n - 1)] \div 2$

centered-polygon numbers are those numbers made by taking e **triangle numbers** of the same size and adding 1. *As with the polygon numbers, their names are determined by the value of e. When the actual shape is made, the 1 goes in the center, and the triangles are arranged around it. Example: When e = 4, then a centered-square number can be made using any four triangle numbers (all the same size) plus 1.*

$C_e(n)$ is used here to indicate a centered-polygon number, using the definitions for n and e as given above. *The value of any centered-polygon number for given values of n and e can be found from the formula*

$$C_e(n) = [en(n - 1) \div 2] + 1$$

The study of polygon numbers goes back as far as 500 BC, but centered-polygon numbers were not devised until the sixteenth century. The fascination has always been in discovering relationships between them (there are many) and inventing other types of "shape numbers." There is no standardized notation for representing any of these numbers.

Polygon numbers and their growth: red shows what is being added each time.

triangle numbers

P₃(1) = 1   P₃(2) = 3   P₃(3) = 6   P₃(4) = 10   P₃(5) = 15

square numbers

P₄(1) = 1   P₄(2) = 4   P₄(3) = 9   P₄(4) = 16   P₄(5) = 25

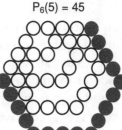

hexagon numbers

P₆(1) = 1   P₆(2) = 6   P₆(3) = 15   P₆(4) = 28   P₆(5) = 45

Centered-polygon numbers and their

centered-triangle numbers:

C₃(1) = 1   C₃(2) = 4   C₃(3) = 10   C₃(4) = 19

centered-square numbers:

C₄(1) = 1   C₄(2) = 5   C₄(3) = 13   C₄(4) = 25

centered-hexagon numbers:

C₆(1) = 1   C₆(2) = 7   C₆(3) = 19   C₆(4) = 37   C₆(5) = 61

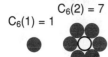

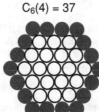
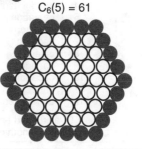

polygons

polygon A polygon is a plane *(= flat)* shape completely enclosed by three or more straight sides. *Usually sides are not allowed to cross one another, and the word is not often used for shapes having fewer than five sides. Polygons are named by the number of sides or angles they have—see table below.*

vertex A vertex is a point where two sides of a **polygon** meet to form a corner.

interior angle An interior angle is the angle formed inside a **polygon** between two adjacent sides.

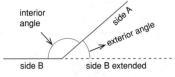

exterior angle The size of an exterior angle at any vertex is
180° minus interior angle *(it may be negative for a concave polygon)*
For ANY polygon the sum of all the exterior angles is 360°.

angle sum The angle sum of a **polygon** is the total of ALL its **interior angles** added together. *For a triangle it is 180°; for a quadrilateral 360°*
Angle sum of any polygon = (180° × number of sides) − 360°

equilateral An equilateral **polygon** is one whose sides are all the same length.

equiangular An equiangular **polygon** is one whose **interior angles** are all the same size.

isogon ≡ **equiangular polygon**

regular A regular **polygon** is one which is both **equilateral** and **equiangular**.

concave A concave **polygon** is one having at least one **interior angle** which is greater than 180°.

convex A convex **polygon** is one whose **interior angles** are all less than 180°. *All regular polygons are convex.*

circumcircle The circumcircle to a polygon is a circle around the OUTSIDE of a **polygon** passing through ALL its vertices. *It is always possible to draw a circumcircle for any regular polygon, but it may not be possible for an irregular polygon and it is never possible for a concave polygon.*

incircle An incircle to a polygon is a circle drawn INSIDE a **polygon** that touches ALL its sides. *It is always possible to draw an incircle for any regular polygon, but it may not be possible for an irregular polygon.*

Table of data for **regular** polygons					
No. of sides	Name	Area = $S^2 \times ...$	C-radius = $S \times ...$	I-radius = $S \times ...$	Interior angle °
3	triangle	0.4330	0.5774	0.2887	60
4	quadrilateral	1	0.7071	0.5	90
5	pentagon	1.7205	0.8507	0.6882	108
6	hexagon	2.5981	1	0.8660	120
7	heptagon	3.6339	1.1524	1.0383	128.57
8	octagon	4.8284	1.3066	1.2071	135
9	nonagon	6.1818	1.4619	1.3737	140
10	decagon	7.6942	1.6180	1.5388	144
11	undecagon	9.3656	1.7747	1.7028	147.27
12	dodecagon	11.196	1.9319	1.8660	150

C-radius and I-radius refer to the circumcircle and incircle respectively.
s is the length of one side. Inexact values are given to 5 significant figures.

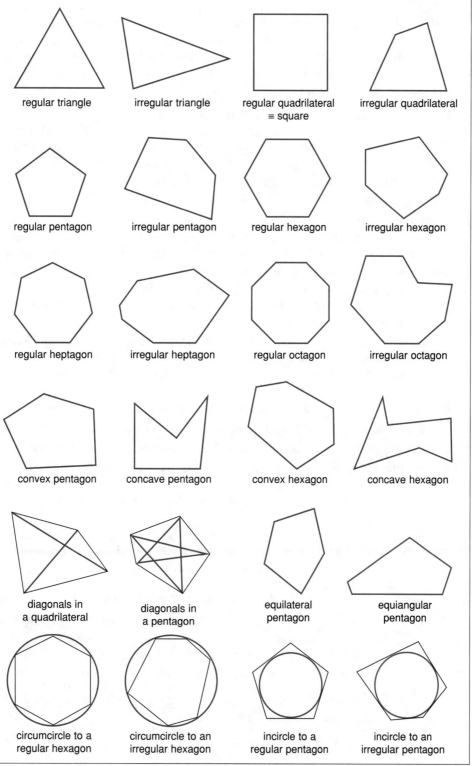

regular triangle | irregular triangle | regular quadrilateral ≡ square | irregular quadrilateral

regular pentagon | irregular pentagon | regular hexagon | irregular hexagon

regular heptagon | irregular heptagon | regular octagon | irregular octagon

convex pentagon | concave pentagon | convex hexagon | concave hexagon

diagonals in a quadrilateral | diagonals in a pentagon | equilateral pentagon | equiangular pentagon

circumcircle to a regular hexagon | circumcircle to an irregular hexagon | incircle to a regular pentagon | incircle to an irregular pentagon

polyhedron A polyhedron is a 3-dimensional shape whose faces are all **polygons**. *It must have at least 4 faces. Its name is based on the number of faces it has. Example: A tetrahedron has 4 faces, a pentahedron has 5 faces, and so on.*

edge An edge is a straight line formed where 2 faces of a **polyhedron** meet.

vertex A vertex of a **polyhedron** is the angular point where 3 or more **edges** meet.

net A net is an arrangement of polygons connected at their edges, all lying in one plane *(= flat surface)* which can be folded up to make a **polyhedron**. *There is always more than one way of doing this. It is also known as a "development."*

convex A convex polyhedron is one in which any straight line joining one **vertex** to another lies entirely on or inside the polyhedron.

nonconvex A nonconvex polyhedron is one which is not **convex**.

regular A regular polyhedron has all of its faces identical, and the same number of **edges** meeting at each **vertex**. *There are only 9 possibilities, of which 5 are convex. These 5 are known as the* **Platonic solids**. *See table below.*

semiregular A semiregular polyhedron is a **polyhedron** of which every face is a **regular polygon** and every **vertex** is identical. *Excluding prisms and antiprisms, there are only 13 possibilities and these are known as the* **Archimedean solids**.

deltahedron A deltahedron is a **polyhedron** whose every face is an **equilateral triangle**. *There are only eight possibilities of the convex type. Three of these are the regular tetra-, octa-, and icosa- hedrons. The other five are irregular and have 6, 10, 12, 14, or 16 faces.*

hexahedron A hexahedron is a **polyhedron** having 6 faces.

cube A cube is a regular **hexahedron** and all its faces are squares.

rectangular solid A rectangular solid is a **hexahedron** whose faces are all rectangles.

circumsphere A circumsphere is the sphere which can be drawn around the OUTSIDE of a **polyhedron** so as to touch all its vertices. *It is always possible to draw a circumsphere for a regular convex polyhedron, but it may not be possible for others.*

insphere An insphere is the sphere which can be drawn INSIDE a **polyhedron** so as to touch all its faces. *It is always possible to draw an insphere for a regular convex polyhedron, but it may not be possible for others.*

Table of data for **regular convex polyhedrons**					
No. of faces	Name	Area = $e^2 \times \dots$	Volume = $e^3 \times \dots$	C-radius = $e \times \dots$	I-radius = $e \times \dots$
4	tetrahedron	1.73205	0.117851	0.612372	0.204124
6	cube	6	1	0.866025	0.5
8	octahedron	3.46410	0.471405	0.707107	0.408248
12	dodecahedron	20.6458	7.66312	1.40126	1.113516
20	icosahedron	8.66025	2.18170	0.951057	0.755761

Area is total surface area of the polyhedron.
C-radius and I-radius refer to the circumsphere and insphere respectively.
e is the length of one edge. Inexact values are given to 6 significant figures.

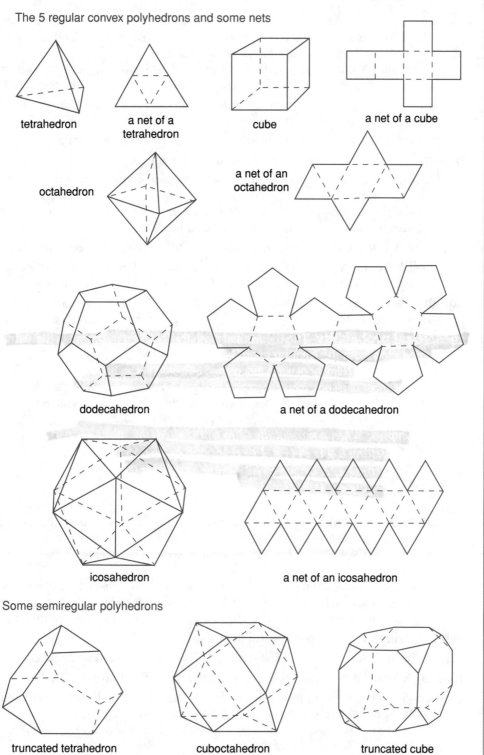

The 5 regular convex polyhedrons and some nets

tetrahedron

a net of a tetrahedron

cube

a net of a cube

octahedron

a net of an octahedron

dodecahedron

a net of a dodecahedron

icosahedron

a net of an icosahedron

Some semiregular polyhedrons

truncated tetrahedron

cuboctahedron

truncated cube

probability

event An event is EITHER an activity OR some specific result of that activity. *Usually it is the second meaning which is intended in* **probability**, *and in that case it is better to use the word* **outcome**. *Example: Rolling a single die is an event (first meaning), and a result of that activity (getting a 1, 2, 3, 4, 5, or 6) is also an event (second meaning).*

outcome An outcome is the actual result of some activity. *It is identical to the second meaning of* **event** *given above.*

frequency The frequency of an **outcome** is the number of times it happens.

possibility A possibility is an **outcome** that CAN happen.

probability The probability of an **outcome** (or event) is a measure of how likely that outcome is. *A value of 0 means it is impossible, while 1 means it is certain; otherwise the value must lie between 0 and 1. It may be given as a common fraction, a decimal fraction, or a percentage.*

P( ) or **Pr( )** is the symbol for the **probability** of the **outcome** named in brackets.

probability scale A probability scale is a line numbered 0 to 1 or 0% to 100% on which **outcomes** (or events) can be placed according to their **probability**.

equally likely A set of **outcomes** associated with a particular activity are described as being equally likely when each occurs as readily as any other.

theoretical probability The theoretical probability of an **outcome** is the value predicted from the fraction given by:

$$\frac{\text{Number of ways that named outcome(s) can happen}}{\text{Number of all possible outcomes which can be obtained from that activity}}$$

This can only be done when the item(s) on which the activity is based (dice, cards, coins, etc.) have outcomes which are all equally likely.
Examples: When a normal die (1 to 6) is rolled, the probability of
getting a 4 is $P(4) = \frac{1}{6}$ or 0.166666 or 16.666 %
getting 1, 2, or 5 is $P(1,2,5) = \frac{3}{6}$ or 0.5 or 50%
getting a 7 is $P(7) = 0$

experimental probability The experimental probability of an **outcome** is the value found after an activity has been done several times and is given by:

$$\frac{\text{Number of times that named outcome(s) did happen}}{\text{Number of times activity was done}}$$

Examples: A thumbtack might be thrown several times and a count made of whether it landed "point up" or "point down." Or a **biased** *die might be rolled many times to determine the experimental probability of getting a 5*

relative frequency ≡ **experimental probability**

fair A fair item (dice, etc.) is one for which all **outcomes** are **equally likely**.

biased A biased item is one in which all **outcomes** are NOT **equally likely**.

chance The chance of an **outcome** might refer EITHER to its being determined only by a whim of fate OR to the **probability** of that outcome. *Examples: "Whether a coin lands heads or tails is a matter of chance."* *"The chance of getting a head is one-half."*

mutually exclusive events are sets of **events** or **outcomes** for which the happening of one means that none of the others can happen.

Example: The outcomes of rolling a die are mutually exclusive, since when one number comes to the top it must mean that none of the others can.

independent events Two or more **events** or **outcomes** are independent if the happening of one has no effect on the other.

Example: When two dice are rolled there are two independent outcomes, since the number showing on one does not influence the number on the other.

dependent events Two **events** or **outcomes** are dependent if a statement or probability for one of them affects a statement or probability for the other.

Example: One box holds 4 red and 6 black marbles; another holds 1 red and 9 black marbles. The probability of choosing a red marble from one box must depend on which box is chosen.

combined events describe the putting together of two or more separate **events** or **outcomes** to be considered as one single event or outcome. *This is usually done in order to find the probability of a final single outcome. The separate outcomes might be independent of, or dependent upon, each other. Examples: Rolling 2 dice (or 1 die twice) and adding the separate scores is combining 2 independent outcomes. Taking 2 crayons from a bag of mixed colors WITHOUT replacing the first is combining 2 dependent outcomes.*

compound events ≡ **combined events**

conditional probability is the **probability** of an **outcome** happening when it is **dependent** upon, or following, some other outcome.

Example: A bag contains 8 red and 2 black marbles. The probability of drawing 2 red marbles, if the first one drawn is not replaced, is given by the probability of the first marble being red times the probability of the second being red, which is $\frac{8}{10} \times \frac{7}{9} = \frac{28}{45}$

tree diagrams are drawn to find and display all possible results when several outcomes are being combined.

Example: When 3 coins are tossed, all possible results can be found and displayed by using a tree diagram like that on the right (H=head, T=tail).

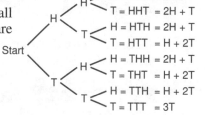

odds are another type of **probability** and the odds against a successful **outcome** happening are given by:

number (of *other* outcomes in the activity) TO number (of ways outcome can happen)

Example: The odds against getting a 3 with a single die are 5 to 1, since there are 5 other numbers and only one 3, so there are 5 ways of losing against only 1 way of winning. The probability of getting a 3 is $\frac{1}{6}$ *or* $\frac{1}{5+1}$

Odds of a to b change to a probability of $\dfrac{b}{(a+b)}$

A probability of $\frac{a}{b}$ changes to odds of $(b-a)$ to a

evens When the **odds** are 1 to 1, they are even. *The probability for evens is $\frac{1}{2}$*

pyramid A pyramid is a **polyhedron** having any polygon as one face with all the other faces being triangles meeting at a common vertex. *The pyramid is named after the polygon forming the face from which the triangles start.*

base The base of a **pyramid** is the polygonal face which names the pyramid.

apex The apex of a **pyramid** is the vertex at which the triangular faces meet.

height The height of a **pyramid** is the distance of its **apex** above the plane of its **base**.

Volume of pyramid = Area of base × Height ÷ 3

altitude ≡ height

vertex In the case of a **pyramid**, vertex is often used to mean the **apex**.

right pyramid A right pyramid is one having all its triangular faces equal in size. *The base is a regular polygon, the apex is perpendicularly above the center of the base, and all the triangular faces make the same angle with the base.*

right square-based pyramid A right square-based pyramid is a **right pyramid** having a square base. *It is what is usually meant when only the word "pyramid" is used and is the type seen in Egypt as a tomb of the Pharaohs.*

oblique pyramid An oblique pyramid is a NON-**right pyramid**.

slant height The slant height of a **pyramid** is the length of a perpendicular from the midpoint of a base-edge to the apex. *The slant heights of a right pyramid are all the same length.*

slant edge The slant edges of a **pyramid** are all those edges joined to the **apex**. *The slant edges of a right pyramid are all the same length.*

frustum of a pyramid A frustum of a pyramid is the part of a **pyramid** cut off between the **base** and a plane which is parallel to the base.

Volume of frustum $= (A + B + \sqrt{AB}) \times h \div 3$ where
A,B = areas of top and bottom faces of frustum
h = distance between faces

cross section A cross section of any 3-D shape is the 2-D figure shown when that shape is cut across, in some specified place and direction, by a plane.

prism A prism is a **polyhedron** having two faces identical and parallel to each other (usually referred to as the ends or bases), and any plane cut made parallel to the ends produces a cross section the same shape and size as the ends. *All faces, other than the ends, are rectangles or parallelograms. Prisms are named after the shape of the end (if it has a name), as in triangular prism or hexagonal prism. If the other faces are rectangles, it is also referred to as a* **right prism**.

The volume of a prism can be found by multiplying the area of one of the end faces by the perpendicular distance between the two ends.

antiprism An antiprism is a **polyhedron** that has two faces identical and parallel to each other. All the other faces are identical triangles, with each vertex of every triangle in contact with a vertex of one of the end faces, so that 4 edges meet at every vertex. *Unlike a prism, its cross section varies.*

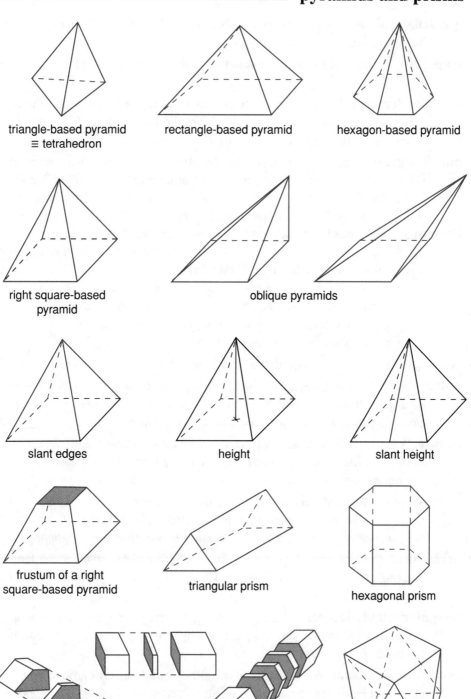

triangle-based pyramid
≡ tetrahedron

rectangle-based pyramid

hexagon-based pyramid

right square-based
pyramid

oblique pyramids

slant edges

height

slant height

frustum of a right
square-based pyramid

triangular prism

hexagonal prism

some prisms and their cross sections

square antiprism

quadrilateral A quadrilateral is a **polygon** which has 4 sides. *Its 4 interior angles add up to 360 degrees.*

trapezoid A trapezoid is a **quadrilateral** which has only one pair of parallel sides.

isosceles trapezoid An isosceles trapezoid is a **trapezoid** in which the two opposite sides, which are not parallel, are the same length. *It has one line of symmetry, and both diagonals are the same length.*

parallelogram A parallelogram is a **quadrilateral** that has two pairs of parallel sides; usually one pair is longer than the other pair and no angle is a right angle. *Usually it has no lines of symmetry. It has rotational symmetry of order 2, and its diagonals bisect each other.*

rhombus A rhombus is a **quadrilateral** whose sides are all the same length, and usually no angle is a right angle. *Its diagonals bisect each other at right angles and both are also lines of symmetry.*

> The area of a trapezoid, parallelogram, or rhombus can be found by adding together the lengths of one pair of parallel sides, dividing by 2, and multiplying the result by the perpendicular distance between them.

rectangle A rectangle is a **quadrilateral** in which every angle is a right angle.

oblong An oblong is a **rectangle** in which one pair of sides is longer than the other pair. *It has two lines of symmetry and rotational symmetry of order 2. Both diagonals are the same length and bisect each other.*

square A square is a **rectangle** whose sides are all the same length. *It has four lines of symmetry and rotational symmetry of order 4. Both diagonals are the same length and bisect each other at right angles.*

kite A kite is a **quadrilateral** that has two pairs of adjacent sides (= *sides which are next to each other*) of the same length, and no angle is bigger than 180 degrees. *It has one line of symmetry and its diagonals cross each other at right angles.*

arrowhead An arrowhead has two pairs of adjacent sides of the same length and ONE angle bigger than 180 degrees. *It has one line of symmetry and its diagonals do not cross.*

irregular quadrilateral Strictly speaking, an irregular quadrilateral is any **quadrilateral** that is not a square, but it is usually taken to be one not having a special name.

cyclic quadrilateral A cyclic quadrilateral is a **quadrilateral** around which a circle can be drawn to pass through all its vertices (= *corners*). *The opposite angles of a cyclic quadrilateral add up to 180 degrees. Rectangles and isosceles trapezoids are always cyclic quadrilaterals; the kite and irregular quadrilaterals sometimes are.*

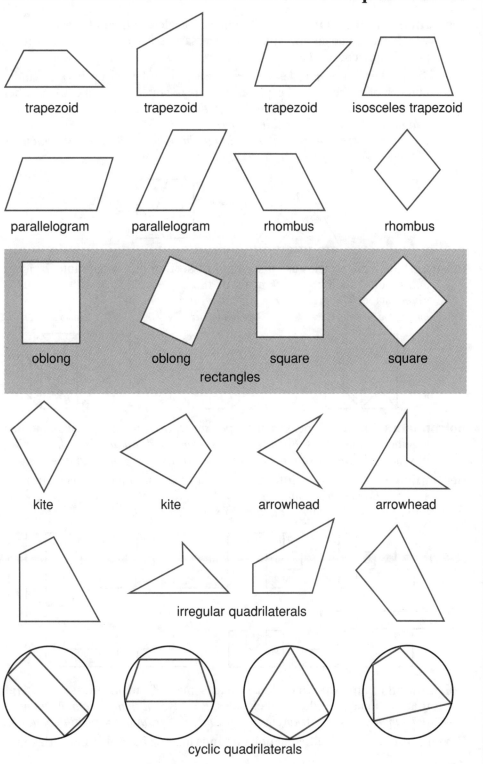

trapezoid   trapezoid   trapezoid   isosceles trapezoid

parallelogram   parallelogram   rhombus   rhombus

oblong   oblong   square   square

rectangles

kite   kite   arrowhead   arrowhead

irregular quadrilaterals

cyclic quadrilaterals

recreational mathematics

recreational mathematics covers games, puzzles, and similar activities in which mathematical principles are necessary in some way: to create them, play them, or solve them.

dissections Dissection puzzles require one shape to be cut up into a definite number of pieces and the pieces then reassembled to make some other shape. *In some cases the pieces are given and the puzzle is to find how they can be used to make a certain shape.*
Example: Dissect an equilateral triangle into the smallest possible number of pieces that can be rearranged to make a square.

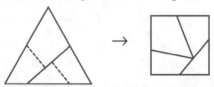

tangram Tangram puzzles use a standard **dissection** of a square into 7 pieces and require finding arrangements of those pieces which will make up a given shape. *The given shape is shown only in outline.*

Making the tangram pieces   A tangram puzzle …   … and its solution

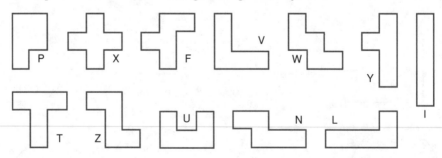

polyominoes are two-dimensional shapes made from identical squares joined together by their sides. *Each type takes its particular name from the number of squares it uses: 4 squares = tetromino; 6 squares = hexomino; etc.*

pentominoes are the 12 different **polyominoes** that can be made from 5 squares. *Each piece is identified by a letter, as shown below. One puzzle for these pieces is to make a rectangle using all 12 of them.*

polyiamonds are two-dimensional shapes made from identical equilateral triangles joined together by their sides. *Each type is named from the number of triangles it uses: 4 triangles = tetriamond; 5 triangles = pentiamond; etc.*

hexiamonds are the 12 different **polyiamonds** that can be made from 6 triangles.

polycubes are three-dimensional shapes made from identical cubes joined together by their faces.

Soma cubes are the 7 different **polycubes** that can be made from 3 or 4 cubes, with each having at least one concave corner. *It takes 27 cubes to make them. The 7 Soma cubes can be assembled to make models of a wide variety of objects. They can be used to make a cube in 240 different ways.*

Examples:

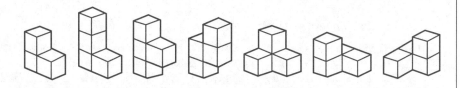

alphametics are problems of an arithmetical type in which all the digits have been replaced by letters (each letter always representing the same digit, and each digit always represented by the same letter) and with the resulting arrangement forming real words.

```
  S E N D
+ M O R E
M O N E Y
```

asterithms are problems of an arithmetical type in which some of the digits have been replaced by asterisks, and the puzzle is to find the correct values of the missing digits.

```
  *   4 6
+ 2   8 *
  4   * 1
```

magic square A magic square is a set of numbers arranged in the form of a square so that the total of every **row**, **column**, and **diagonal** is the same. *Usually every number must be different. In most cases the numbers also form a sequence of some sort or other.* Examples:

8	3	4
1	5	9
6	7	2

16	2	3	13
5	11	10	8
9	7	6	12
4	14	15	1

using primes only

17	89	71
113	59	5
47	29	101

Latin square A Latin square of size *n* by *n* is one in which *n* different objects are each repeated *n* times and arranged in a square array so that none of them is repeated in any row or column.

Greco-Latin square A Greco-Latin square is made by combining two **Latin squares** (each of which is made of a different set of objects) so that no PAIR of objects is repeated. *Squares of this type are very useful in the design of experiments.* Example:

A	B	C	D
C	D	A	B
D	C	B	A
B	A	D	C

+

1	2	3	4
4	3	2	1
2	1	4	3
3	4	1	2

=

A1	B2	C3	D4
C4	D3	A2	B1
D2	C1	B4	A3
B3	A4	D1	C2

sequence A sequence is a set of numbers or objects made and written in order according to some mathematical rule.

term A term is one of the separate numbers or objects of a **sequence**. *The terms of a sequence are usually separated by a comma and a space.*

random sequence A random sequence is a set of numbers or objects made and written in order, according to NO apparent rule and for which, no matter how many **terms** are known, the next cannot be predicted with certainty.

natural numbers The natural number sequence is that **sequence** which is used for counting.
The series begins (10 terms shown): 1, 2, 3, 4, 5, 6, 7, 8, 9, 10, ...

doubling sequence A doubling sequence is a **sequence** in which each term is twice (× 2) the value of the previous term. *It usually starts with 1*
The series begins (10 terms shown): 1, 2, 4, 8, 16, 32, 64, 128, 256, 512, ...

lucky number sequence The lucky number sequence is made from the **natural numbers** by first deleting every second number; from those that are left delete every third number; from those delete every fourth number; then every fifth, sixth, seventh, and so on until no more can be deleted; those remaining form the sequence. *Rules can be made up for generating all sorts of sequences.*
The series begins (10 terms shown): 1, 3, 7, 13, 19, 27, 39, 49, 63, 79, ...

recursive sequence A recursive sequence is a **sequence** in which each new **term** is defined in relation to some terms which have been made previously.

Fibonacci sequence The Fibonacci sequence is a **recursive sequence** where, starting with the first two terms as 1, 1, each new term is made by adding together the two previous terms.
The series begins (10 terms shown): 1, 1, 2, 3, 5, 8, 13, 21, 34, 55, ...
Formally this is written as $F_n = F_{n-2} + F_{n-1}$ where $F_1 = 1$ and $F_2 = 1$
The value of the nth term can be found from the formula:

$$F_n = \frac{1}{\sqrt{5}} \left(\frac{1 + \sqrt{5}}{2} \right)^n \quad \text{rounded to the nearest whole number}$$

Lucas sequence The Lucas sequence is a **recursive sequence** where, starting with the first two terms as 1, 3, each new term is made by adding together the two previous terms.
The series begins (10 terms shown): 1, 3, 4, 7, 11, 18, 29, 42, 71, 113, ...
Formally this is written as $L_n = L_{n-2} + L_{n-1}$ where $L_1 = 1$ and $L_2 = 3$

arithmetic progression or **AP** An AP is a **sequence** where each new **term** after the first is made by ADDING a constant amount to the previous term.
Example: 3, 7, 11, 15, 19, ... with a first term of 3 and a constant of 4.

geometric progression or **GP** A GP is a **sequence** where each new **term** after the first is made by MULTIPLYING the previous term by a constant amount.
Examples: 2, 6, 18, 54, 162, ... with a first term of 2 and a constant of 3
14, 7, 3.5, 1.75, 0.875, ... with a first term of 14 and a constant of 0.5

series A series is a **sequence** with addition signs placed between the **terms**. *It is possible to use subtraction by treating it as the addition of a negative term.*

arithmetic series An arithmetic series is an **AP** with addition signs inserted.
Example: Using the previous AP, the series is 3 + 7 + 11 + 15 + 19 + …
To find the sum (total) of an arithmetic series over *n* terms, use the formula

$$na + n(n-1)d \div 2$$ where

a is the value of the first term
n is the number of terms
d is the constant added to each term

geometric series A geometric series is a **GP** with addition signs inserted.
To find the sum (total) of a geometric series over *n* terms, use the formula

$$\frac{a(r^n - 1)}{r - 1}$$ where

a is the value of the first term
n is the number of terms
r is the constant multiplier

convergent series A convergent series is a **series** which, as more and more terms are used, moves toward some definite value.

divergent series A divergent series is a **series** which, no matter how many terms are used, never settles to a definite value.

alternating series An alternating series is a **series** whose terms are alternately positive (+) and negative (–).

infinite series An infinite series is a **series** with an unlimited number of terms. *However many terms exist, it is always possible to make one more.*

π An **alternating series** which is **infinite** and **converges** is

$$\frac{1}{1} - \frac{1}{3} + \frac{1}{5} - \frac{1}{7} + \frac{1}{9} - \frac{1}{11} + \frac{1}{13} - \frac{1}{15} + \dots$$

It converges to the value of $\frac{\pi}{4}$ *so it can be used to calculate the value of π, but it converges so slowly that it takes over 100,000 terms to give the value correct to only 5 decimal places. Another series, which is quicker, is*

$$\frac{\pi^4}{96} = \frac{1}{1^4} + \frac{1}{3^4} + \frac{1}{5^4} + \frac{1}{7^4} + \frac{1}{9^4} + \frac{1}{11^4} + \dots$$

This one is correct to 4 decimal places with only 10 terms, but there are other series, as well as other methods, which are much quicker than that.

trigonometric functions The trigonometic functions are a group of **functions** (identified as sine, cosine, etc.) each of which maps the size of any angle to a real number. *This is done by expressing each of the functions as an infinite series. The series for the sine, cosine, and tangent functions are given. The angle x has to be expressed in* **radians**.

$$\sin x = x - \frac{x^3}{3!} + \frac{x^5}{5!} - \frac{x^7}{7!} + \frac{x^9}{9!} - \dots$$

$$\cos x = 1 - \frac{x^2}{2!} + \frac{x^4}{4!} - \frac{x^6}{6!} + \frac{x^8}{8!} - \dots$$

$$\tan x = x + \frac{x^3}{3} + \frac{2x^5}{15} + \frac{17x^7}{315} + \frac{62x^9}{2835} + \dots$$

set A set is a collection of objects (letters, numbers, symbols, etc.) which is defined EITHER by listing all the objects OR by giving a rule that allows a decision to be made as to whether or not an object belongs in that set. *Sets are usually listed or defined within curly brackets:{ }.*

> *Examples: {a, e, i, o, u} is a listed set that could also be described by the rule {the vowels}.*
>
> *{5, a person, a table, Z} is a listed set for which a rule would be difficult to find.*
>
> *{all the numbers} is a rule for a set that it is impossible to list.*

universal set The universal set is the **set** which is first defined (by list or rule) and within which all the statements that follow must be interpreted.

> *Examples: After the universal set {positive numbers less than 10} is given, the set {even numbers} would be only {0, 2, 4, 6, 8}.*
>
> *In the universal set {all positive numbers} $x = \sqrt{4}$ has only the solution $x = 2$, since $^-2$ is not in the universal set.*

U is the symbol for the **universal set**.

universe ≡ **universal set**

member A member of a **set** is one of the objects contained in that set.

element ≡ **member**

∈ is the symbol meaning "is a member of."

> *Example: $2 \in$ {even numbers}*

empty set The empty set is the **set** which has NO **members**.

> *Example: The set {all odd numbers divisible by 2} is empty.*

∅ is the symbol for the **empty set**.

null set ≡ **empty set**

subset A subset is a **set** which contains part of (or all of) another set.

⊂ is the symbol meaning "is a subset of."

> *Example: {2,7, f, t, M, ϕ} $\subset$ {numbers, letters, symbols}*

proper subset A proper subset is a **subset** which does NOT contain ALL the members of the other set.

complement The complement of a **set** is all those **members** which are NOT in that set, but which ARE in the **universal set** originally given.

′ is the symbol for the complement of a **set**.

> *Example: Suppose the universal set is {odd numbers less than 30} and the set A is {all prime numbers}*
>
> *Then the complement of A is shown by A′ and is {1, 9, 15, 21, 25, 27}*

union The union of two (or more) **sets** is their combination into a single set containing ALL the **members** of the original sets. *If a member is found more than once in the original sets, then it is shown only once in the union.*

∪ is the symbol for the **union** of sets.

> *Example: {4, 7, 13, 20} $\cup$ {2, 7, 10} is {2, 4, 7, 10, 13, 20}*

intersection The intersection of two (or more) **sets** is the single set made containing ONLY **members** commonly found in all the original sets.

$\cap$ is the symbol for the **intersection** of sets.
Example: {4, 7, 13, 20} $\cap$ {2, 7, 10} is { 7}

disjoint Disjoint **sets** are those having NO **members** in common.

superset If A is a **subset** of B, then B is said to be a superset of A.

$\supset$ is the symbol meaning "includes" or "is a superset of."
Example: A $\supset$ B can be read as "set A includes set B" or "set A is a superset of set B" or "set B is a subset of set A."

symmetric difference The symmetric difference of two **sets** is the single set made which contains only **members** which were found ONCE in the original sets. *A member found in both sets would not be included.*

∇ is the symbol for the **symmetric difference** of two sets.
Example: {2, 5, 8, 12} ∇ {1, 5, 12, 15} is {1, 2, 8, 15}

Venn diagrams are used to give a pictorial view of the relationships of **sets** and **subsets** within a **universal set**; the universal set is shown enclosed by a rectangle, and all others by circles or simple closed curves.
Examples:

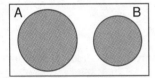

2 subsets (A and B) within a
universal set
A and B are disjoint

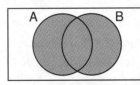

A ∪ B
union of A and B

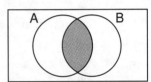

A ∩ B
intersection of A and B

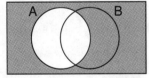

A' = complement of A

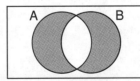

A ∇ B
symmetric difference of A and B

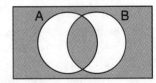

(A ∇ B)'
complement of symmetric
difference of A and B

finite set A finite set is a **set** whose **members** can be counted.

infinite set An infinite set is a **set** whose **members** cannot be counted and the quantity cannot be stated in terms of any defined number.
Example: The set of all real numbers is an infinite set.

enumerate To enumerate a **set** (or **subset**) is to list all its **members**.

denumerable A denumerable **set** is one for which a mapping can be established which puts all its members into a one-to-one correspondence with the positive integers.

space and shapes

2-D or **two-dimensional space** A space is described as being two-dimensional if, to give the position of any point in that space, two and only two measurements are necessary from a pair of nonparallel straight lines fixed in that space.

3-D or **three-dimensional space** A space is described as being three-dimensional if, to give the position of any point in that space, three and only three measurements are necessary from three straight lines (no pair being parallel) fixed in that space.

shape A shape is made by a line or lines drawn on a surface, or by putting surfaces together. *It is usual in mathematics to require that the lines or surfaces be closed in such a way that an inside and an outside of the shape can be defined. When a shape is named it needs a context to determine whether it is the enclosed space that is being referred to or its defining outline.*
Example: Circle may refer either to the line defining it or to the shape enclosed by that line.

solid A solid is a **shape** formed in **three-dimensional space**. *The most common of these are the: cube, rectangular solid, cylinder, cone, pyramid, prism, and sphere.*

edge An edge of a **shape** is the line, or one of the lines, defining the outline of that shape. *In three-dimensional shapes the edges are usually formed where the defining surfaces meet.*

face A face is a plane surface enclosed by an **edge** or edges.

side is used to refer to the **edge** of a two-dimensional shape.

vertex A vertex of a shape is a point at which two or more **edges** meet. *It is more commonly referred to as a corner.*

diagonal A diagonal of a shape is a straight line which joins one **vertex** to another vertex and which is NOT an edge of that shape.

face diagonal A face diagonal of a three-dimensional shape is a **diagonal** which lies entirely in one **face** of the shape.

space diagonal A space diagonal of a three-dimensional shape is a **diagonal** which is NOT a **face diagonal**.

perimeter The perimeter of a **two-dimensional shape** is the total distance around the sides defining the outline of that shape. *Example: The perimeter of the shape on the right is found by adding together the lengths of the 4 sides marked a, b, c, and d.*

circumference ≡ **perimeter** of a circle or an ellipse.

rectilinear shape A rectilinear shape is a **two-dimensional shape** whose **sides** are all straight lines. *All polygons are rectilinear shapes.*

parallelepiped A parallelepiped is a **solid** having 6 faces each of which is a parallelogram. *Opposite faces are parallel. A rectangular solid is a special case of a parallelepiped where each of the faces is a rectangle.*
Volume = Area of 1 face × Perpendicular distance between *that* face and the one opposite

$v = 3 \times 4 = 12$
$12 \times 5 = 60$

rhombohedron A rhombohedron is a **parallelepiped** whose faces are rhombuses.

dimension A dimension of a shape is one measurement taken between two specific points on the outline of the shape or, in some cases, inside the shape. *Usually several dimensions are needed to fix the size of a shape.*

length
breadth
width
height
depth
thickness

These are all commonly used labels to indicate positions for which the **dimensions** of a shape are given or needed. Conventional usage is:
* length for a single dimension
* length and breadth (or width) for two dimensions with length being the greater, plus
* height, depth, or thickness when a third dimension is needed.
However, these labels are often used much more loosely.
Example: The three main dimensions of a cupboard are generally referred to as its width, depth, and height.

area The area of a surface is a measure of how much two-dimensional space is covered by that surface. *It is usually measured in terms of how many squares of some unit size (square inches, square meters, etc.) would cover an equivalent amount of space.*

volume The volume of a three-dimensional shape is a measure of how much space is contained within, or occupied by, that shape. *It is usually measured in terms of how many cubes of some unit size (cubic inches, cubic meters, etc.) would fill an equivalent amount of space.*

tessellation A tessellation is an arrangement of shapes which fit together to fill a space. *There must be NO gaps. The word is most commonly applied to the filling of two-dimensional space, but it also applies to three-dimensional space. Additional requirements are often made that the shapes used are identical and that the pattern used in the filling could be continued indefinitely.*

tiling A tiling is a **tessellation** in two-dimensional space which uses only a single repeated shape. *Any triangle, quadrilateral, or regular hexagon can be used to make a tiling as well as a wide variety of other shapes. Examples are:*

 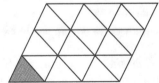 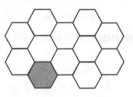

rep-tile A rep-tile (≡ replicating tile) is a two-dimensional shape of which multiple copies can be put together to make another shape which is **similar** to the original. *The simplest shapes with which this can be done are the right-angled isosceles triangle and a rectangle (or parallelogram) whose edges are in the ratio 1: $\sqrt{2}$. A more complex example is shown on the right. Many other rep-tiles can be found.*

statistics involves the collection, display, and analysis of information. *Usually the information is numerical in type or else is changed into a numerical form.*

data is the complete set of individual pieces of information which is being used in any of the processes connected with **statistics**.

raw data is the **data** as it was originally collected, before any processing at all has been done.

grouped data is **data** that has been put into groups according to some particular rules to make it easier to handle. *It is most often grouped according to size. Example: Collecting data about the heights of 100 people could result in 100 different measurements. It is easier to handle if the data is put into groups. Suitable groups might be: less than 100; 100–120; 120–140; 140–160; 160–180; 180–200; over 200 (all in cm). That is very simple but still needs decisions as to where a piece of data at the end of a group goes. For instance, to which group does a person of height 160 cm belong? For greater precision this is done by writing the class interval as falling between two inequalities such as "140 < height ≤ 160 cm." In this case the first and last groups would be "height < 100 cm" and "height > 200 cm."*

class A class of data is one of the groups in a collection of **grouped data**.

class limits are the two values which define the two ends of a **class** and between which the data must lie.

class interval The class interval is the width of a **class** as measured by the difference between the **class limits**. *In any collection of grouped data the class intervals are very often all the same but do not have to be. Common exceptions are the classes at each end when arranged in size order.*
Example: Under "grouped data" the example uses definite class intervals of 20 cm except for the first and last classes (or groups), which are open.

discrete data is **data** which can only be of certain definite values.
Example: A survey of shoe sizes being worn by a group of people would use discrete data, since there are only a limited amount of values for the sizes in which shoes are made and sold.

continuous data is **data** which can take any value within certain restrictions. *The restrictions might be the class limits if the data is grouped; or those of the measuring device when the data is collected; or those of common sense. Example: A survey of lengths of people's feet involves continuous data. They can be of any length, but the usual measuring instruments do not record beyond 3 decimal places, and common sense dictates that there are certainly both upper and lower limits to what we might expect to find.*

frequency The frequency of some **data** is the number of times each piece of that data is found.

f is the symbol for **frequency**.

population A population is the complete set of objects (values or people) which is being studied by some statistical method.

distribution The distribution of a set of **data** is a graph or table showing how many pieces of data there are in each **class**, or of each type.
Example: This table shows the distribution of shoe sizes among 100 women:

Shoe size	5	6	7	8	9	10
Number of women	14	20	35	18	9	4

normal distribution A normal distribution is one in which the **frequency diagram** is symmetrical about a line through the mean value (which is also the median and the mode), and has a shape like that shown on the right. *The curve (known as a bell curve) is derived from a particular formula. It really needs a lot of data to produce something that approximates to a curve, but the phrase is loosely used for frequency diagrams that seem to have that rough general shape.*

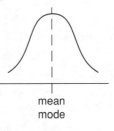

mean
mode

skewed distribution A skewed distribution is one in which the **frequency diagram**, while having a single mode, is not symmetrical about the mean.

positively skewed A distribution is said to be positively skewed if the **mode** lies to the LEFT of the **mean** (mode < mean) in the frequency diagram.

negatively skewed A distribution is said to be negatively skewed if the **mode** lies to the RIGHT of the **mean** (mode > mean) in the frequency diagram.

dispersion The dispersion of a set of **data** is a measure of the way in which the **distribution** is spread out. *There are various ways it can be measured, but the one most often used is known as the **standard deviation**.*

spread ≡ **dispersion**

modal class The modal class of a set of **grouped data** is the **class** which has the greatest **frequency**.

bimodal A set of **grouped data** is said to be bimodal when the **distribution** (shown graphically) has two separate and distinct peaks.
Example: The drawing on the right shows a distribution which is bimodal.

two-way table A two-way table is a table of data which shows the combined effect of two separate happenings. *On the right is a two-way table which shows (in red) the combined total scores possible when two dice are rolled. From this table it can be seen that, with two dice, a score of 7 can happen in more ways than any other score, while 2 and 12 can happen in only one way.*

+		Second die				
	1	2	3	4	5	6
1	2	3	4	5	6	7
2	3	4	5	6	7	8
3	4	5	6	7	8	9
4	5	6	7	8	9	10
5	6	7	8	9	10	11
6	7	8	9	10	11	12

(First die along the left column)

statistics (graphical)

frequency diagram A frequency diagram is a graphical way of showing the amount of **data** found in each of the groups or types being counted.

bar chart A bar chart is a **frequency diagram** using rectangles of equal width whose heights or lengths are proportional to the frequency. *Usually adjacent rectangles or bars touch each other only if the data is continuous; for discrete data a space is left between the bars. The bars may be of any width and sometimes are no more than lines.*

block graph A block graph is a **bar chart** in which, usually, the bars themselves are divided to mark off each individual piece of data.

histogram A histogram is a **frequency diagram** using rectangles whose widths are proportional to the **class interval** and whose areas are proportional to the frequency. *The class intervals may or may not be of equal width; if they are of equal width, then the histogram is indistinguishable from a bar chart.*

pictogram A pictogram is a **frequency diagram** using a symbol to represent so many units of data. *The symbol usually relates to the data being shown.*

stem and leaf plot A stem and leaf plot is a **frequency diagram** which displays the actual data together with its frequency, by using a part of the value of each piece of data to fix the class or group (the stem), while the remainder of the value is actually listed (the leaves).

pie chart A pie chart is a circular **frequency diagram** using sectors whose angles at the center are proportional to the frequency.

scattergram A scattergram shows how two sets of numerical **data** are related, by treating matching pairs of numbers as coordinates and plotting them as a single point, repeating this as necessary for each data-pair.

correlation is an assessment of how strongly two pieces of **data** appear to be connected to the extent that a change in one of them must produce a change in the other. *This assessment is usually made after a scattergram has been drawn. It can vary from being nonexistent through weak to very strong.*

positive correlation is a **correlation** in which an INCREASE in the value of one piece of data tends to be matched by an INCREASE in the other.

negative correlation is a **correlation** in which an INCREASE in the value of one piece of data tends to be matched by a DECREASE in the other.

line of best fit The line of best fit is the **trend line** drawn on a **scattergram**. *The higher the correlation, the easier it is to draw this line.*

cumulative frequency is the total of all the **frequencies** of a set of **data** up to any particular piece or group of data.

cumulative frequency diagram or **polygon** A cumulative frequency diagram is a diagram on which all the various **cumulative frequencies** are plotted, each against the data value for which it has been calculated. *The points may be joined by straight lines (when it is usually called a polygon) or, if there are sufficient points to define it, by a curve.*

Bar chart showing shoe sizes of 100 women

Block graph showing colors of 20 cars

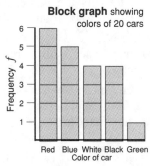

Histogram showing numbers of people in age groups

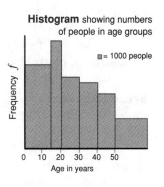

= 1000 people

Pie chart showing shoe sizes of 100 women

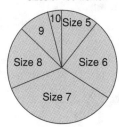

Pictogram showing total number of computers owned in each class

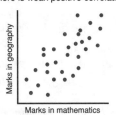

Class 1
Class 2
Class 3
Class 4
Class 5

= 5 students

Stem and leaf plot using the tens digit as the stem and the units as the leaves to show the data set:

1, 3, 12, 14, 14, 17, 20, 23, 25, 28, 29, 31, 36, 37

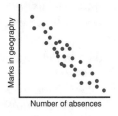

Scattergram showing marks gained in 2 tests by 30 students. There is NO correlation.

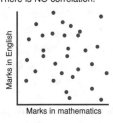

Scattergram showing marks gained in 2 tests by 30 students. There is weak positive correlation.

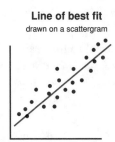

Scattergram showing marks against number of absences for 30 students. There is strong negative correlation.

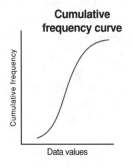

Line of best fit drawn on a scattergram

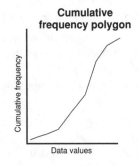

Cumulative frequency polygon

Cumulative frequency curve

range The range of a set of **data** is the numerical difference between the smallest and the greatest values to be found in that data.
> *Example: For the data 9, 3, 3, 15, 11, the range is 15 – 3 = 12*

measures of central tendency of a set of **data** are any values about which the **distribution** of the data may be considered to be roughly balanced.

arithmetic mean The arithmetic mean of a set of **data** is the numerical value found by adding together all the separate values of the data and dividing by how many pieces of data there are. *It is a measure of central tendency.*
> *Example: For the data 9, 3, 3, 15, 11, the arithmetic mean is 41 ÷ 5 = 8.2*

mean The mean value of a set of **data** is usually taken to be the **arithmetic mean**.

$\bar{x}$ is the symbol for the **arithmetic mean**.

average An average of a set of **data** is any **measure of central tendency**. *Usually it is taken to be the same as the* **arithmetic mean**.

weighted mean The weighted mean of a set of **data** is the **mean** value found after each piece of data has been multiplied by some factor which gives a measure of its importance or its **frequency** of happening.
> *Example: This table shows the distribution of shoe sizes among 100 women:*

Shoe size	5	6	7	8	9	10
Number of women	15	19	35	18	8	5

> *The mean shoe size could be given as (5+6+7+8+9+10) ÷ 6 = 7.5 but this does not allow for the fact that some sizes are a lot more common than others. The weighted mean size is*
> *[(5 × 15) + (6 × 19) + (7 × 35) + (8 × 18) + (9 × 8) + (10 × 5)] ÷ 100 = 7*

working mean A working mean is an assumed value for the **mean** of a set of **data**. *The use of a working mean allows other calculations to be done as the data is being entered and a correction made once the true mean is known.*

median The median value of a set of **data** is the numerical value of the piece of data in the middle of the set, AFTER THE SET IS ARRANGED IN SIZE ORDER. *If there is an even number of pieces of data, the* **mean** *of the middle two is taken as the median.*
> *Example: Data 9, 3, 3, 15, 11 has a median of 9 (middle of 3, 3, 9, 11, 15), while 6, 2, 12, 4, 7, 18 has a median of 6.5 (mean of middle pair 6 and 7).*

mode The mode of a set of **data** is that data which is found most often.
> *Example: Data 9, 3, 3, 15, 11 has a mode of 3 (since 3 occurs most often).*

percentile When a set of data is arranged in size order, the *n*th percentile is the value such that *n*% of the data must be less than or equal to that value; and *n* must be a whole number from 1 to 99. *Percentiles should be used only with large sets of data so that dividing it up into 100 equal parts (as percentiles implies) seems realistic.*
> *Example: When the data (arranged in size order) is the set of measurements 3.7   4.5   7.3   8.3   8.4   9.6   10.1   10.8   11.6   12.4 cm, then the 30th percentile is 7.3 but that data set is unrealistic for percentiles.*

lower quartile The lower quartile of a set of data is the 25th **percentile**. *One quarter (25%) of all the data must have a value that is less than, or equal to, the value of the lower quartile.*
Example: For the data given under "percentile" the lower quartile must be midway between the 20th and 30th percentile, which is (4.5 + 7.3) ÷ 2 = 5.9 cm.

upper quartile The upper quartile of a set of data is the 75th **percentile**. *Three-quarters (75%) of all the data must have a value that is less than, or equal to, the value of the lower quartile.*
Example: For the data given under "percentile" the upper quartile is 11.2 cm.

interquartile range The interquartile range of a set of data is the difference in value between the **lower** and **upper quartiles** for that data. *It is one way of measuring the dispersion of the data.*
Example: The interquartile range for the above data is 11.2 – 5.9 = 5.3 cm.

semi-interquartile range is one-half of the **interquartile range**.
Example: The previous example has a semi-interquartile range given by
$$5.3 \div 2 = 2.65 \ cm.$$

deviation The deviation of a value is the difference between that value and some other value. *The other value is usually the mean or median of the data.*

mean deviation The mean deviation of a set of **data** is the mean distance between the value of each piece of data and some fixed value. *The fixed value is usually the mean of all the data, but it can be the median. All the distances are considered to be positive.*

standard deviation The standard deviation of a set of **data** is a measure of its **dispersion** and is found by carrying out this calculation:
> Find the difference in value between each piece of data and the mean of all the data.
> Square all the differences *(this makes them all positive)*.
> Add them together and divide by how many there are.
> Take the square root.

Many calculators have a key that allows this procedure to be carried out automatically once the data has been entered.
*Example: Using the data for shoe sizes given under **weighted mean** and working from the mean of 7, the calculation is:*
$$[(^-2^2 \times 15) + (^-1^2 \times 19) + 0 + (1^2 \times 18) + (2^2 \times 8) + (3^2 \times 5)] \div 100 = 1.74$$
(The multiplications allow for the frequency of each piece of data.)
So the standard deviation is $\sqrt{1.74}$ = 1.32 (to 3 sf)

variance The variance of a set of **data** is a measure of its **dispersion**. Its value is given by the square of the **standard deviation**. *It can also be said that the standard deviation is the square root of the variance.*
Example: In the previous example the variance is 1.32^2 = 1.74

σ (the Greek letter sigma) and s are symbols used for the **standard deviation**.
σ *is used when it is for the whole population, s is used for a sample.*

σ^2 and s^2 are symbols used for the **variance**.

box and whisker diagram A box and whisker diagram (also called a **boxplot**) is a drawing which displays seven measures relating to one set of data. *The diagram must be matched to a relevant number line, which is usually the horizontal axis of the associated frequency diagram. The numerical values of the measures may, or may not, be written in as well. It is a useful pictorial summary for comparing sets of data.*
Example: This box and whisker diagram (drawn in red) summarizes the data concerning the heights of a group of people.

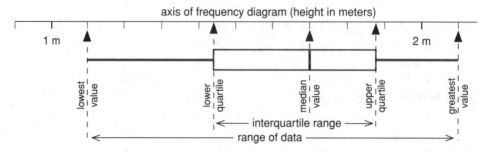

axis of frequency diagram (height in meters)

moving average A moving average is used to smooth out the fluctuations in value of a set of data which varies widely over time. It is made by reevaluating the mean of the last few pieces of data whenever a new piece of data is added to the list. *It is used to give a clearer idea of the underlying trend.*
Example: A shop's recorded weekly sales of pencils might be:

8	10	6	11	4	9	9	6	5	10

which, by taking three-week moving averages, gives this smoother looking set:

8	9	7	8	7.3	8	6.7	7

Notice that each value of the moving average is placed at the end of the group of 3 pieces of data for which it has been calculated. The effect is most marked when the data is plotted on a graph. This is done on the right, where the black line is for the raw data and the red line shows the moving average. There is a clear indication that sales are decreasing.

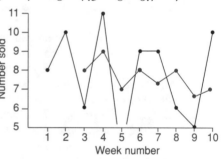

correlation coefficient is a measure of the linear association between two variables. The value of the correlation coefficient always lies in the range $-1 \leq r \leq 1$. *If an increase in one variable is closely matched by an increase in the other variable, the correlation coefficient will be close to 1. If an increase in one variable is closely matched by an decrease in the other variable, the correlation coefficient will be close to -1. When there is no linear correlation, the correlation coefficient will be zero.*

sample A sample is a set chosen from a **population** and used to represent that population in the statistical methods being applied. *This is necessary where it is not possible to collect all the data from a very large population.*
Example: In an opinion poll to see how people would vote in an election, it is possible only to ask a sample of the population about their intentions and predict a result for the whole population from that.

random A result (of some event) is said to be random if, from all the results that could happen as a consequence of that event, each result has the same chance of happening and, no matter how many results have already been found, the next cannot be predicted.

random selection A random selection is any process by which objects (or numbers) are chosen in such a way that the appearance of each object is **random**. *The process might be rolling a fair die, reading numbers from a printed random number table, or drawing marbles from a bag, provided that the marbles are replaced and the bag is well shaken between each drawing. Computers and calculators usually have a routine for generating random numbers, although, strictly speaking, these should be called pseudo-random, since the routine must depend upon a known algorithm.*

random sample A random sample is a **sample** that has been chosen by a process of **random selection** so that it models the characteristics of the **population** it is supposed to represent as closely as possible.

systematic sampling is the method used to produce a **sample** from a **population** which is arranged in some order. *The order might be actual or implied, as with birth dates.*
Example: From a list of 30 names, or a street of 30 houses, it is desired to choose one-third of them as a sample. Taking every third name or house would be a systematic way of producing the sample of 10.

stratified sampling is done by dividing the population to be sampled into groups, or strata, according to some criterion, and taking appropriate samples (random or systematic) from each of those groups. These separate samples are then put together to make a stratified sample of that population. *Commonly used criteria are age, sex, social class, and occupation.*

quota sampling is done by deciding in advance how many of the population, in each of certain categories, are to be chosen. *The quotas are often set to represent how many of each category are known to be present in the total population.*
Example: A survey about attitudes among older people might specify that, from the over-60 population, 100 men and 125 women are to be questioned.

sampling error is the difference between the **mean** of the **sample** and the mean of the **population** from which that sample was drawn. *It is important to have some idea of the probable size of this error in order to assess how much confidence can be placed in any conclusions made, based on the sample.*

structure The structure of a system first defines the objects to be used and then the way in which they are to be used. *The structure dealt with here is mainly that for arithmetic and the objects are numbers, but the general ideas and definitions are applicable to many other parts of mathematics.*

operation An operation is a rule (or body of rules) for processing one or more objects. *The most basic operations of arithmetic are those of addition, subtraction, multiplication, and division, and the objects being processed are numbers. In mathematics generally the operations can be much more complex and the objects are usually algebraic in form.*

operator An operator is the symbol used to show which **operation** is to be done.
Examples: $+ \; - \; \times \; \div$ are all operators.

set Before any **operation** can be used, it is necessary to make clear on what **set** of objects it is to be used.
Examples: The set might be "all whole numbers" or "only positive numbers" or "real numbers" or "quadratic equations," and so on.

binary operation A binary operation is an **operation** which combines two objects to produce a third. *Addition, subtraction, multiplication, and division are all binary operations, since they all require two numbers from which a third number is made.*

unary operation A unary operation is an **operation** requiring only one object to work on from which it produces another. $\sqrt{}$ *is a unary operator.*

closed An **operation** on a particular **set** is said to be closed if the operation always produces a result that is also in the set.
Examples: Addition on numbers is closed, since number + number = number. Multiplication is also closed. Subtraction on positive numbers is not closed, since it is possible to get a negative result which is not in the set. Division on integers is not closed, because fractions are excluded.

commutative A commutative **operation** is one in which the order of operating on the two objects does not matter.
Examples: Addition is commutative, since $3 + 5 = 5 + 3$. Subtraction is NOT *commutative, since $6 - 4 \neq 4 - 6$*

associative A **binary operation** is said to be associative if, when it is being applied repetitively, the result does not depend on how the pairs are grouped (whether by working or by the insertion of brackets).
Examples: Addition is associative, since $1 + 2 + 3 = (1 + 2) + 3$ OR $1 + (2 + 3) = 6$. Subtraction is not associative, since $5 - 4 - 2$ might be EITHER *$5 - (4 - 2) = 3$ OR $(5 - 4) - 2 = {}^{-}1$ producing two different results.*

identity The identity for a **binary operation** on a **set** is an object in that set which, when combined (by the operation) with a second object from the set, produces a result which is equal to the second object.
Examples: Addition of numbers has the identity 0, since $0 + 5 = 5$
Multiplication of numbers has the identity 1, since $1 \times 7 = 7$
This is generally expressed as $0 + x = x + 0 = x$ and $1 \times x = x \times 1 = x$

left or **right identity**   A left identity or a right identity is an **identity** which works only on the nominated (left or right) side of the other object.
Examples: Subtraction of numbers has a right identity of 0, since $x - 0 = x$ but no left identity, since $0 - x \neq x$. Division has a right identity of 1

inverse   The inverse of an object in a **set** under a **binary operation** is another object which, when combined with the inverse, produces the **identity** as the result.
Example: For numbers under addition any number x has the inverse ^-x since $x + {}^-x = 0$ (the identity for addition).

group   A group is a **set** under a **binary operation** for which ALL the following statements are true:
>The operation is **closed**.
>The operation is **associative**.
>The set has an **identity**.
>Every object in the set has an **inverse**.

Example: Integers are a group under addition but not under multiplication, since inverses (= fractions) do not exist within the set.

commutative group   A commutative group is a **group** with the extra property that the operation is **commutative**.

Abelian group ≡ **commutative group**

distributive law   The distributive law (if it is applicable) describes how two operators may be used together when linked in a particular way.
Example: The distributive law of arithmetic says that multiplication is distributed over addition, as in $a \times (b + c) = a \times b + a \times c$

modulus   The modulus of a particular system of arithmetic is an integer value which is used as a divisor throughout that system.

mod   is an abbreviation for modulo, which is used to identify the number being used as the **modulus**.
Example: When the modulus is 4, the system is working modulo 4 or mod 4

residue   The residue of any number is the remainder after that number has been divided by a specified **modulus**.
Example: Using a modulus of 4, the residue of 7 is 3; or $7 \equiv 3 \pmod 4$.

congruent   Two numbers are said to be congruent if they both have the same **residue** when the same **modulus** is used.
Example: 7(mod 4) and 15(mod 4) both have a residue of 3, so 7 is congruent to 15(mod 4).

≡   is the symbol for "is congruent to." *Examples: $7 \equiv 3 \pmod 4$; $7 \equiv 15 \pmod 4$.*

modular arithmetic   is a system of arithmetic based on relating numbers to each other only by their **residues** for some given **modulus**.
Example: A multiplication table (mod 4) is shown. It is not a group, since there are no inverses for 0 and 2: both $0 \times x = 1$ and $2 \times x = 1$ have no solution.

×	0	1	2	3
0	0	0	0	0
1	0	1	2	3
2	0	2	0	2
3	0	3	2	1

symbols

A symbol is a letter or sign used to represent instructions, or a number, in a more concise form. Sometimes a symbol replaces a group of words and can be read directly as it occurs, in these cases the words are shown below in "quotation marks."

+	"add" or "positive"	
−	"minus" or "subtract" or "negative"	
×	"times" or "multiplied by"	
*	"times" or "multiplied by"	*Usually used on a computer*
÷	"divided by" or "shared by"	*Example: 6 ÷ 3 or 6/3 both mean "6 divided by 3"*
/	"divided by" or "shared by"	*or "6 shared by 3" or "How many 3's in 6?"*
±	"add or subtract" "plus or minus" "positive or negative"	*Example: When x = 3 then x ± 2 gives the two answers 5 and 1* *±6 means the two numbers +6 and ⁻6*
=	"equals" or "is equal to"	*Example: x + 3 = 7*
≠	"does not equal" or "is not equal to"	
≈	"is approximately equal to"	*Example: π ≈ 3.14*
≡	"is equivalent to" or "has the same value as"	*Example: $5.00 ≡ 500¢*
≡	"is identically equal to"	*Example: $(x + y)^2 ≡ x^2 + 2xy + y^2$*
<	"is less than"	*Example: x < 5 means x can take any value which is less than 5 but cannot equal 5*
≤	"is less than or equal to"	*Example: x ≤ 7 means x can take any value which is less than 7 or may equal 7*
>	"is greater than"	*Example: x > 3 means x can take any value which is greater than 3 but cannot equal 3*
≥	"is greater than or equal to"	*Example: x ≥ 6 means x can take any value which is greater than 6 or may equal 6*
∝	"varies as" or "is proportional to"	*Example: y ∝ x means that y changes in some regular way as x changes.*
.	decimal point	*It is placed on the line and used to separate the whole number part from the fractional part.*
,	decimal marker	*Example: 3,48 is equivalent to 3.48* *The comma is standard in the SI or metric system.*
%	"percent" or "out of a hundred"	
‰	"per mil" or "out of a thousand"	
[x]	the largest whole number which is not greater than x	*Example: [3.5] is 3, but [−4.2] is ⁻5*
|x|	absolute value; the value of x with no sign attached	*Example: |⁻8.7| is 8.7*
x^2	"x squared" or "x multiplied by itself"	*Example: $4^2 = 4 × 4 = 16$*
x^3	"x cubed"	*Example: $2.5^3 = 2.5 × 2.5 × 2.5 = 15.625$*

$\sqrt{x}$ "the positive square root of x"   *Example:* $\sqrt{9} = 3$, *since* $3 \times 3 = 9$

$\sqrt[3]{x}$ "the cube root of x"   *Example:* $\sqrt[3]{8}$ $= 2$, *since* $2 \times 2 \times 2 = 8$

$\angle$ "angle"   *Example:* $\angle ABC$ *or* $\angle B$

$\parallel$ "is parallel to"   *Example:* $AB \parallel CD$

$\perp$ "is perpendicular to"   *Example:* $AB \perp CD$

$\llcorner$ these lines are at right angles to each other

Examples:

°   "degree"   *of angle or temperature*

′   "minute"   *one-sixtieth of a degree or an hour*

″   "second"   *one-sixtieth of a minute (of angle or time)*

$n\,!$ "factorial n"   *Multiply together all the integers from 1 to n*

$\{\,\}$ used to enclose a listed set   *Example:* $\{A, B, C, D, E, F\}$

$\in$ "is a member of"   *Example:* $D \in \{A, B, C, D, E, F\}$

$\notin$ "is not a member of"   *Example:* $X \notin \{A, B, C, D, E, F\}$

$\subset$ "is a subset of"   *Example:* $\{A, D, E\} \subset \{A, B, C, D, E, F\}$

$\supset$ "includes"   *Example:* $\{A, B, C, D, E, F\} \supset \{A, D, E\}$

$\cup$ union of two sets   *Example:* $\{A, D\} \cup \{B, C, D, E\}$
$$\equiv \{A, B, C, D, E\}$$

$\cap$ intersection of two sets   *Example:* $\{A, C, D\} \cap \{B, C, E\} \equiv \{C\}$

$\varnothing$ null or empty set   *Example:* $\{A, D\} \cap \{B, C, E\} \equiv \{\} \equiv \varnothing$

σ standard deviation

$\Rightarrow$ "implies"

$\Leftarrow$ "is implied by"

$\Leftrightarrow$ "implies and is implied by"   *also written as* iff

$\therefore$ "therefore"   *Example:* $AB \perp CD \therefore \angle ABC = 90°$

∞ "infinity"

e ≈ 2.71828

$f(x)$ "a function of x"   *Example:* $f(x)$ *is* $x^2 + 3x - 4$

π pi ≈ 3.14159

$(\,)$ parentheses

$[\,]$ square brackets

$\{\,\}$ curly brackets

Parentheses or **brackets** are used (in pairs) to enclose an expression that is to be treated as a complete quantity and evaluated before the rest of the expression. Brackets can be nested within each other, and the use of different types allows matching pairs to be seen more readily.
Example: $4\{5x[2x(x+5) - 7]+8\} - 17$ *is* $40x^3 + 200x^2 - 40x - 13$

symmetry Symmetry applied to any object (or situation) means that parts of the object correspond to (or match) other parts in some way.

symmetry of shape The symmetry of a shape describes how parts of that shape can, under certain rules of movement, fit exactly on to other parts of the same shape. There are three types of shape symmetry: line, rotational, and plane.

line symmetry is the **symmetry** of a plane shape *(= flat or 2-D shape)* which can be folded along a line so that one half of the shape fits exactly on the other half. *A shape can have several lines of symmetry.*
Examples with lines of symmetry shown in red:

rotational symmetry is the **symmetry** of a shape which may be turned and fitted on to itself somewhere other than in its original position.
Examples with centers, about which the shape is turned, shown in red:

center of symmetry The center of symmetry is the point about which a shape having **rotational symmetry** is turned.

point symmetry ≡ rotational symmetry

order of rotational symmetry The order of rotational symmetry of a shape counts the number of times that a shape can be turned to fit on to itself until it comes back to its original position. *Every shape has an order of rotational symmetry of at least 1, but this is usually ignored. In these examples the letters are used only to show the positions of the shape as it turns.*

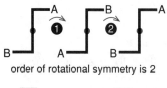

order of rotational symmetry is 2   order of rotational symmetry is 3

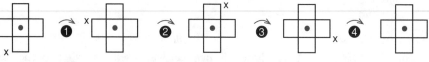

Note how marking a shape in some way can change its order of rotational symmetry. The cross above is of order 4, but the one on the right (with color added) is of order 2.

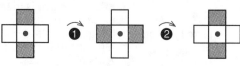

plane symmetry is the **symmetry** of a three-dimensional shape in which a plane *(= flat)* mirror can be placed so that the reflection looks exactly the same as the part of the shape being covered up by the mirror. *A shape can have several planes of symmetry.*
Examples, with planes of symmetry shown in red, are:

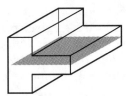 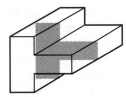

bilateral symmetry $\Big\}$ $\Big\{$ all of these are the same as either
mirror symmetry $\quad$ **line symmetry** in two dimensions
reflective symmetry $\quad$ or **plane symmetry** in three dimensions.

asymmetric A shape having NO **symmetry** at all is described as asymmetric.
Examples of shapes that are asymmetric are

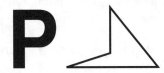 

axis of symmetry An axis of symmetry of a shape is a line about which the shape can be rotated, by an amount which is less than a whole turn, so that the total effect is to leave the shape unchanged. *A shape can have more than one axis of symmetry. In the case of line symmetry the line is the axis; for rotational symmetry the axis is a line passing through the center of symmetry and perpendicular to the plane of the shape.*

axis of rotation An axis of rotation is a line about which a shape or another line is turned.

symmetric expression A symmetric expression is an algebraic expression using two or more variables whose value is unchanged if any two of the variables are interchanged.
Examples: $x + y$ $\qquad$ $x^2 + y^2$ $\qquad$ $x^2 + y^2 + z^2 + xyz$

symmetric equation A symmetric equation is an **equation** using a **symmetric expression**.
Examples: $x + y = 6$ $\qquad$ $x^2 + y^2 = 10$ $\quad$ $x^2 + y^2 + z^2 + xyz = 104$

symmetric function A symmetric function is a **function** using a **symmetric expression**. *Such functions when drawn as graphs will show some form of symmetry.*
Examples: $f(x) \equiv x + y$ $\quad$ $f(x) \equiv x^2 + y^2$ $\quad$ $f(x) \equiv x^2 + y^2 + z^2 + xyz$

symmetric relation A symmetric relation is a relationship which is true (or false) whichever way it is read. *The most commonly encountered symmetric relation is the equals sign, since if $x = y$, then $y = x$. Another is "is parallel to," since if AB is parallel to CD, then CD is parallel to AB.*

techniques

algorithm An algorithm is a step-by-step procedure that produces an answer to a particular problem. *Many algorithms are prepared ones which do the standard operations needed in an efficient or the most memorable way: multiplication, division, adding fractions, etc. Other algorithms are devised as they are needed, particularly for computers.*

proportionality constant A proportionality constant is a fixed value, often represented by k, which is determined for a given pair of quantities and then applied to find an unknown quantity of a pair with the same relationship. *Example: A car goes 480 miles on 30 gallons of gasoline (this is the given pair of quantities). How much gasoline would be needed for a trip of 1000 miles? The computation on the right shows how the proportionality constant k is determined, and how it is used to find the unknown quantity.*

$$y = kx$$
$$480 = 30\,k$$
$$k = 16$$
$$y = 16x$$
$$1000 = 16x$$
$$x = 62.5 \text{ gallons}$$

proportion Setting up a proportion is a technique which can be used to solve the same type of problem described above. The quantities are written in a prescribed order and an equation is formed by multiplying the first and fourth terms (the EXTREMES) and setting them equal to the product of the second and third terms (the MEANS).
Example: Using the same problem given for proportionality constant, the proportion and solution would be written out as:

$$480 : 30 :: 1000 : x$$
$$480x = 3000$$
$$x = 62.5 \text{ gallons}$$

laws of exponents are those rules which control the operations of combining numbers written in exponent notation. These laws can be applied only to numbers in exponent form which have the same base.

With a base of b and exponent values of m, n then

$$b^m \times b^n = b^{m+n} \qquad b^m \div b^n = b^{m-n} \qquad (b^m)^n = b^{mn}$$

$$b^0 = 1 \qquad\qquad b^{-n} = \frac{1}{b^n}$$

Examples: $2^3 \times 2^5 = 2^8 \qquad 2^3 \div 2^7 = 2^{-4} \qquad (2^3)^5 = 2^{15} \qquad 2^{-3} = \frac{1}{2^3} = \frac{1}{8}$

iteration An iteration is a procedure which is repeated many times so that, from an estimated solution to a particular problem, each repeat produces a better approximation to the solution. *These solutions are usually numbered by means of a subscript, as in $x_1 \quad x_2 \quad x_3 \quad x_4 \quad \dots \quad x_n \quad x_{n+1}$ etc.*
Example: An iterative formula to find the cube root of a number (N) is:

$$x_{n+1} = \sqrt{\sqrt{N \times x_n}}$$

Given $N = 4$ and starting with $x_1 = 1$ then $x_2 = 1.4142\dots$ $x_3 = 1.5422\dots$ $x_4 = 1.5759\dots$ and so on to $x_{13} = 1.587401\dots$ which is accurate to 6 decimal places.

cross-multiplication is a method of simplifying an equation involving fractions based on the fact that $\frac{a}{b} = \frac{c}{d} \Leftrightarrow ad = bc$.

Example: $\frac{2}{5} = \frac{4}{x} \Leftrightarrow 2x = 5 \times 4$ so $x = 10$

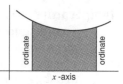

area under a curve The area under a curve is the area enclosed between a curve drawn on a coordinate grid, two limiting **ordinates**, and the *x*-axis. *The three principal methods of finding it (apart from counting squares) are given below.*

midordinate rule The midordinate rule is a method for finding the approximate area under a curve by dividing the space into strips; finding the areas of the separate strips by multiplying the length of the middle ordinate of each strip by the width of that strip; and finally adding the areas of the strips together. *It is a practical method that can be used when the equation of the curve is not known.*

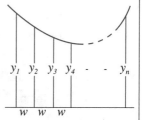

trapezoidal rule The trapezoidal rule is a method for finding the approximate area under a curve which is similar to the midordinate rule but treats each strip as a **trapezoid**. *It can be very accurate if the strips are made as narrow as is practicable. By using strips of equal widths, one can reduce the whole procedure to a formula.*

If the width of each strip is w and the lengths of the ordinates are y_1 y_2 y_3 ... y_n, then the area is given by:
$$w \left[\tfrac{1}{2} (y_1 + y_n) + y_2 + y_3 + y_4 + \ldots y_{n-1}\right]$$

Simpson's rule is a method for finding the approximate area under a curve by dividing the space between the limiting ordinates into an even number of equal-width strips. *It is usually more accurate than the previous methods.* With ordinates numbered from 1 to n (n being odd), the area is given by:
Width $\times$ [4 $\times$ Sum of even ordinates + 2 $\times$ Sum of odd ordinates – (First + Last)] $\div$ 3
With any of these methods, if the equation of the curve is known, the lengths of the ordinates (the y-values) can be calculated, rather than measured, for the greatest accuracy.

linear programming is a method used to find the "best" solution to problems which can be expressed in terms of linear equations or inequalities. *Solutions are usually found by drawing graphs of inequalities and looking for optimum values that satisfy the required conditions. This method is widely used in business and industrial contexts, and the problems often relate to obtaining maximum profits for given costs and production levels.*

solving quadratics If a quadratic equation can be put in the form $ax^2 + bx + c = 0$, then it can be solved, and its roots found, by using the formula on the right.
$$x = \frac{-b \pm \sqrt{b^2 - 4ac}}{2a}$$

difference of two squares Any algebraic expression of the form $a^2 - b^2$ can be factored into $(a + b)(a - b)$.
Example: $x^2 - 9$ is $x^2 - 3^2$, which is $(x + 3)(x - 3)$

temperature The temperature of something is a measure of how hot it is according to a value given on a known scale. *Temperature is measured by means of a thermometer or similar instrument. When heat moves between objects it always moves from an object at a higher temperature to an object at a lower one. There are three main scales used for measuring temperature.*

Celsius scale The Celsius scale sets the freezing point of water at zero degrees (≡ 0°C) and the boiling point at 100 degrees (≡ 100°C).
The system was devised by Anders Celsius (1701–1744), a Swedish astronomer.

Fahrenheit scale The Fahrenheit scale sets the freezing point of water at 32 degrees (≡ 32°F) and the boiling point at 212 degrees (≡ 212°F). *Note that Fahrenheit degrees are smaller than Celsius degrees.*
The system was devised by G. D. Fahrenheit (1686–1736), a German physicist.

To change temperatures between the Celsius and Fahrenheit scales, use either the dual conversion scale on the far right or the conversion graph opposite. For more accuracy, follow one of these flow diagrams:

To change °F to °C use:

To change °C to °F use:

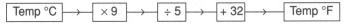

Kelvin scale The Kelvin scale is based on laws of physics in which there is an absolute zero, and all temperatures are measured from that point in units called kelvins, where 1 kelvin is the same size as 1 degree on the **Celsius scale**. *Note that when temperatures are given in K the ° sign is not used. Since the starting point is absolute zero, there can be no negative temperatures on this scale. In fact, temperatures of less than 0 K (zero kelvin) or its equivalent on any other scale, (–273.15°C or –459.67°F) cannot exist. This scale was devised by William Thomson, First Lord Kelvin (1824–1907), a Scottish physicist and mathematician.*

To change temperatures between the Celsius and Kelvin scales, use:
Temperature in °C = Temperature in K – 273.15
Temperature in K = Temperature in °C + 273.15

centigrade The centigrade scale was the name originally given to the **Celsius scale**. *It was officially changed (in 1948) because it could be confused with a system of angle measurement which used grades and centigrades.*

There were two other scales of note which were used for a while but are now obsolete. One was the Réaumur scale, which was similar to the Celsius scale, with the same zero point but with only 80 degrees to the boiling point of water.
R. A. F. de Réaumur (1683–1757) was a French entomologist.
The other was the Rankine scale, which was similar to the Kelvin scale but based on the size of the Fahrenheit degree.
W. J. M. Rankine (1820–1872) was a Scottish engineer.

conversion graph A conversion graph is used to show the corresponding values between two quantities, which have a fixed relationship between them, by means of a line drawn on a squared grid. *In making a conversion graph the two quantities which are related are marked on a squared grid, using any suitable scales and putting one along each axis. A line is then plotted and drawn to show the relationship between the two quantities so that intermediate values can be read off. The graph below can be used to change temperatures between the Celsius and Fahrenheit scales. The line of red dashes show that the readings of 35°C and 95°F are measuring the same temperature.*

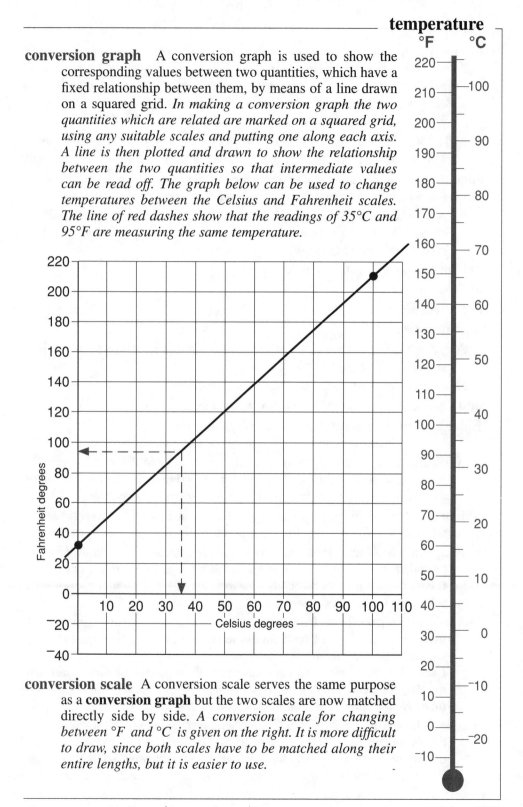

conversion scale A conversion scale serves the same purpose as a **conversion graph** but the two scales are now matched directly side by side. *A conversion scale for changing between °F and °C is given on the right. It is more difficult to draw, since both scales have to be matched along their entire lengths, but it is easier to use.*

topology is the study of shapes and their properties which are not changed by transformations of a particular type. *It is popularly known as "rubbersheet" geometry, since the lines defining the shape may be deformed in all manner of ways but may never be broken or joined as a part of the process. Measurements relating to distance and direction have no place in topology.*

graph A topological graph is made up of a set of points and lines joining them.

vertex A vertex in a topological **graph** is one of the points which make the graph.

edge An edge in a topological **graph** is one of the lines which make the graph, and which must have a vertex at each end.

face A face in a topological **graph** is any single area completely enclosed by **edges**. *The area surrounding the graph, outside its boundary edges, is considered as one of the faces of that graph.*

network ≡ **graph** (of the topological variety)

node ≡ **vertex**

arc ≡ **edge**

region ≡ **face**

order of a vertex The order of a vertex is a number which states how many **edges** are joined to that **vertex**.

even vertex An even vertex is a **vertex** whose **order** is an EVEN number.

odd vertex An odd vertex is a **vertex** whose **order** is an ODD number.

Euler's formula states that in any topological **graph**:

Number of faces + Number of vertices − Number of edges = 2

traversable A topological **graph** is said to be traversable if it can be drawn as one continuous line without going over any **edge** more than once. *Such a graph can only have either no odd vertices or two odd vertices.*

unicursal A topological **graph** is said to be unicursal if it is **traversable** and any start and finish are at the same point. *It will have NO odd vertices.*

topological transformations allow a shape to be deformed in almost any way provided that it always retains the same number of **vertices**, **edges**, and **faces**; the same **order** for all the vertices; the points along each edge following in the same relative positions.

topologically equivalent Two shapes are said to be topologically equivalent if, using only **topological transformations**, one can be deformed in such a way as to become identical to the other.
Example: Bus and train companies often use diagrams that are topologically equivalent to the real layout of the roads and rails, to simplify them. No measurements can be made on such diagrams.

Schlegel diagram A Schlegel diagram is a topological **graph** which represents a **polyhedron**. It is made by representing the polyhedron by its edges and deforming those, using only **topological transformations**, so that it lies flat. *The edges, vertices, and faces of the polyhedron become those of the graph.*

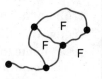

topological graphs with every edge in red, every vertex in black,
and faces marked with an F

odd vertex
of order 1

even vertex
of order 2

odd vertex
of order 3

even vertex
of order 4

traversable graph   a unicursal graph   These two graphs are
topologically equivalent.

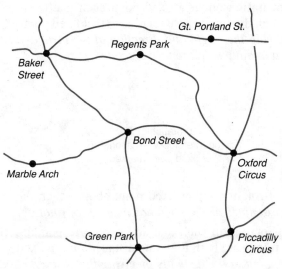 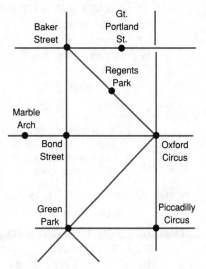

The above shows a topological transformation applied to a railway map with the
actual layout shown on the left and the topologically equivalent diagram on the right.

Schlegel diagrams

  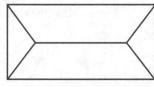

a cube   a tetrahedron   a triangular prism

transformation geometry

transformation A transformation is a change carried out under specific rules.

transformation geometry deals with the operations that may be used on a figure to affect its position, shape, or size; or any combination of those. *The figure may be as small as a single point, and anything larger may be thought of as being made up of many points.*

object The object is the original shape BEFORE a **transformation** is applied.

image The image is the shape which appears AFTER the **transformation** has been applied to the **object**.

translation A translation is a **transformation** such that every point in the **object** can be joined to its corresponding point in the **image** by a set of straight lines which are all parallel and of equal length. *A translation is described by the direction and length of the movement.*
Examples:

rotation A rotation is a **transformation** about a fixed point such that every point in the **object** turns through the same angle relative to that fixed point. *A rotation is described by giving the angle and direction of the turn, and the position of the fixed point about which the turn is made.*
Examples:

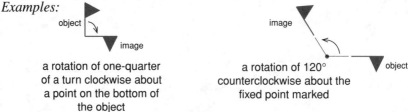

a rotation of one-quarter
of a turn clockwise about
a point on the bottom of
the object

a rotation of 120°
counterclockwise about the
fixed point marked

center of rotation The center of rotation is the fixed point about which the **rotation** takes place. *In the examples above each has a center of rotation.*

reflection A reflection is a **transformation** such that any two corresponding points in the **object** and the **image** are both the same distance from a fixed straight line. *A reflection is fully described simply by giving the position of the fixed line in relation to the object.*

mirror line A mirror line is the fixed line used in making a **reflection**.
Examples: Each of these shows the effect of reflecting an object in the mirror line which is shown as a single black line. Note that, in this case, the words object and image could be interchanged.

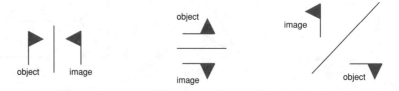

glide reflection   A glide reflection is a **transformation** made by combining a **translation** with a **reflection** whose **mirror line** is parallel to the direction of the translation.
Example: A repeated glide reflection used to make a pattern.

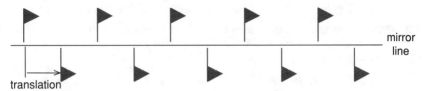

isometry   An isometry is a **transformation** or combination of transformations, such that every distance measured between a pair of points in the **object** is the same as the distance between the corresponding pair of points in the **image**. *The object and image are the same shape and size. The translation, rotation, reflection, and glide reflection are all isometries.*

direct isometry   A direct isometry is an **isometry** in which either no **reflection** or else an even number of them has been used. *Using an odd number of reflections produces an **opposite isometry***.

enlargement   An enlargement is a **transformation** in which the distances between every pair of points in the **object** are multiplied by the same amount to produce the **image**. *The multiplier can take any value— negative, positive, or fractional—but not zero.*
Examples:

scale factor   A scale factor is the value of the multiplier used to make an **enlargement**. *Note that the scale factor is a multiplier for changing lengths only. The multiplier which affects the area will be (the scale factor)^2. For the change in volume of a 3-D shape it is (the scale factor)^3*

center of enlargement   When the **object** and **image** of an **enlargement** have their corresponding points joined by straight lines, then all those lines will cross at a common point called the center of enlargement.

shear   A shear is a **transformation** in which all the lines in the **object** parallel to some fixed line (usually referred to as the base line) are moved in a direction parallel to that line, and an amount which is proportional to their distance from that line. *A shear is not an isometry, but the areas of the object and image are the same.*
Examples:

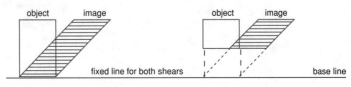

triangle A triangle is a **polygon** which has three sides. *Its three interior angles add up to 180°. Triangles are usually described by reference to their sides or their angles (or both).*

scalene triangle A scalene triangle has ALL its sides of DIFFERENT lengths. *All of its angles must also be of different sizes. It has no symmetry.*

isosceles triangle An isosceles triangle has TWO sides of the SAME length. *Two of its angles must also be of the same size. It has one line of symmetry but no rotational symmetry.*

equilateral triangle An equilateral triangle has ALL of its sides the SAME length. *All its angles are of the same size and equal to 60°. It has three lines of symmetry and rotational symmetry of order 3.*

acute triangle An acute triangle has NO angle GREATER than 90°. *It must also be one of the above types of triangles.*

obtuse triangle An obtuse triangle has ONE angle GREATER than 90°. *It is also either an isosceles or a scalene triangle.*

right-angled triangle A right-angled triangle has ONE angle EQUAL to 90°. *It is also either an isosceles or a scalene triangle.*

hypotenuse The hypotenuse is the side of a **right-angled triangle** which is opposite to the right angle. *It is also the longest side of that triangle.*

base The base of a **triangle** is any side chosen to serve that purpose. *Usually it is the side which is at the "bottom" when the triangle is in a given position.*

altitude The altitude of a **triangle** is the distance between any one side and the vertex opposite to that side, measured along a line which is at right angles to that side. *Any triangle has three altitudes. Their lines (extended if necessary) all cross at the same point.*

height ≡ altitude

median The median of a triangle is a straight line joining one vertex of a **triangle** to the middle of the opposite side. *Any triangle has three medians and they all cross one another at the same point.*

median triangle The median triangle is the one formed by drawing straight lines between the midpoints of the three sides of another triangle. *A median triangle divides the original triangle into four congruent triangles.*

circumcircle A circumcircle to any triangle is the circle around the OUTSIDE of a **triangle** passing through all its vertices.

incircle An incircle to any triangle is the circle drawn INSIDE the **triangle** touching all its sides. *Each side is a tangent to the incircle.*

Area of a triangle = Length of base × Altitude ÷ 2

$$\text{Radius of circumcircle} = \frac{abc}{4 \times \Delta}$$

$$\text{Radius of incircle} = \frac{\Delta}{s}$$

where

a, b, c are lengths of sides
Δ is area of triangle
s is length of semiperimeter
$$s = \frac{a + b + c}{2}$$

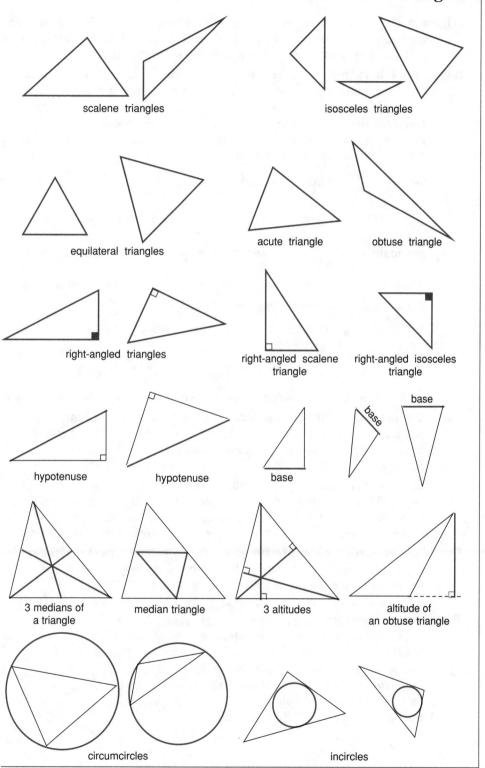

scalene triangles

isosceles triangles

equilateral triangles

acute triangle

obtuse triangle

right-angled triangles

right-angled scalene triangle

right-angled isosceles triangle

hypotenuse

hypotenuse

base

base

base

3 medians of a triangle

median triangle

3 altitudes

altitude of an obtuse triangle

circumcircles

incircles

trigonometry

trigonometry is the study of triangles with regard to their measurements and the relationships between those measurements using **trigonometric ratios**, and also goes on to deal with **trigonometric functions**.

trigonometric ratios express the relationship which exists between the size of one angle and the lengths of two sides in a right-angled triangle.

These ratios can be defined in relation to the standard triangle shown on the right, where A, B, and C are the three angles and a, b, and c are the lengths of the three corresponding sides. There are six of these ratios:

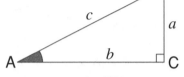

$$\text{sine } A = \frac{a}{c} \qquad \text{cosine } A = \frac{b}{c}$$

$$\text{tangent } A = \frac{a}{b}$$

$$\text{cosecant } A = \frac{c}{a} \qquad \text{secant } A = \frac{c}{b} \qquad \text{cotangent } A = \frac{b}{a}$$

These are usually written as: sin cos tan csc sec cot

Some relationships between these ratios are:

$$\tan A = \frac{\sin A}{\cos A} \qquad\qquad \sin^2 A + \cos^2 A = 1$$

$$\csc A = \frac{1}{\sin A} \qquad \sec A = \frac{1}{\cos A} \qquad \cot A = \frac{1}{\tan A}$$

In any of the fractions given above, none of the bottom values can be zero.

$\mathbf{sin^{-1}}$**...** ≡ **arcsin...** ≡ **inverse sine...** Any of these mean that the size of the angle which corresponds to the number given by "..." is to be found. *Unless otherwise known, this is an angle between ⁻90° and +90° Examples: sin⁻¹ 0.5 is 30° arcsin ⁻0.5 is ⁻30°*

$\mathbf{cos^{-1}}$**...** ≡ **arccos...** ≡ **inverse cosine...** Any of these mean that the size of the angle which corresponds to the number given by "..." is to be found. *Unless otherwise known, this is an angle between 0° and +180° Examples: arccos 0.5 is 60° inverse cosine ⁻0.5 is 120°*

$\mathbf{tan^{-1}}$**...** ≡ **arctan...** ≡ **inverse tangent...** Any of these mean that the size of the angle which corresponds to the number given by "..." is to be found. *Unless otherwise known, this is an angle between ⁻90° and +90° Examples: inverse tangent 0.5 is 26.6° arctan ⁻0.5 is ⁻26.6°*

Pythagoras' theorem In any right-angled triangle, the area of the square drawn on the **hypotenuse** *(= longest side)* is equal to the total area of the squares drawn on the other two sides. *In the diagram, the area of square Z is equal to the areas of square X and square Y added together. In terms of the side lengths a, b, and c as shown in triangle ABC above, the relationship is:*

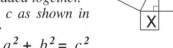

$$a^2 + b^2 = c^2$$

law of sines The law of sines is based on the fact that in any triangle the length of any side is **proportional** to the **sine** of the angle opposite to that side.

$$\frac{a}{\sin A} = \frac{b}{\sin B} = \frac{c}{\sin C}$$

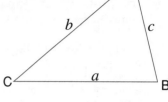

law of cosines The law of cosines is an extension of **Pythagoras' theorem,** which allows it to be applied to any triangle.

$$a^2 = b^2 + c^2 - 2bc \cos A \qquad \text{or} \qquad \cos A = \frac{b^2 + c^2 - a^2}{2bc}$$

sine curve A sine curve is the graph showing how the value of the sine of an angle changes with the size of the angle. *It has an upper bound of 1 and a lower bound of ⁻1*

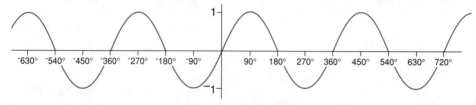

cosine curve A cosine curve is the graph showing how the value of the cosine of an angle changes with the size of the angle. *It has an upper bound of 1 and a lower bound of ⁻1. It is the same as the sine curve shifted left by 90°.*

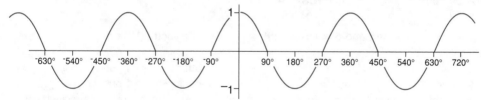

tangent curve A tangent curve is the graph showing how the value of the tangent of an angle changes with the size of the angle. *A tangent graph is drawn on the right.*

periodicity The periodicity of a curve is a measure of the distance a curve goes before it repeats itself. *The sine and cosine curves both have a periodicity of 360° while the tangent curve has a periodicity of 180°.*

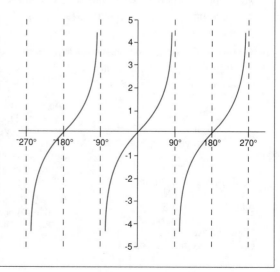

115

units and conversions

There are three main systems of measurement still in use. These are known as: **imperial units,** shown here as (UK), American units shown as (US), and **metric units,** which form the basis of the Système International d'Unités (SI). The units in each of those systems are:

Length (UK and US)

12	inches	≡ 1	foot
3	feet	≡ 1	yard
22	yards	≡ 1	chain
10	chains	≡ 1	furlong
8	furlongs	≡ 1	mile
1760	yards	≡ 1	mile

Length (Metric)

10	millimeters	≡ 1	centimeter (cm)
10	centimeters	≡ 1	decimeter (dm)
10	decimeters	≡ 1	meter (m)
10	meters	≡ 1	decameter (dam)
10	decameters	≡ 1	hectometer (hm)
10	hectometers	≡ 1	kilometer (km)

Area (UK and US)

144	sq inches	≡ 1	square foot
9	sq feet	≡ 1	square yard
4840	sq yards	≡ 1	acre
640	acres	≡ 1	square mile

Area (Metric)

100	sq mm	≡ 1	sq cm (cm^2)
10000	sq cm	≡ 1	sq meter (m^2)
100	sq meters	≡ 1	are (a)
100	ares	≡ 1	hectare (ha)
100	hectares	≡ 1	sq kilometer (km^2)

Volume (UK and US)

1728	cu. inches	≡ 1	cubic foot
27	cu. feet	≡ 1	cubic yard

Volume (Metric)

1000	cu. mm	≡ 1	cu cm (cm^3)
1000	cu. cm	≡ 1	liter
1000	liters	≡ 1	cu meter (m^3)

Mass (UK and US)

437.5	grains	≡ 1	ounce
16	ounces	≡ 1	pound
2000	pounds	≡ 1	short (US) ton
2240	pounds	≡ 1	long (UK) ton

Mass (Metric)

1000	grams	≡ 1	kilogram (kg)
1000	kilograms	≡ 1	tonne (t)

Capacity (UK liquid and dry, US liquid)

4 gills	≡ 1	pint
2 pints	≡ 1	quart
4 quarts	≡ 1	gallon

Capacity (US dry)

2 pints	≡ 1	quart
8 quarts	≡ 1	peck
4 pecks	≡ 1	bushel

Note that UK and US gallons are not the same size, so other measures of capacity having the same name are not the same size. Also a liquid pint is not the same size as a dry pint.

Time

60	seconds	≡ 1	minute
60	minutes	≡ 1	hour
24	hours	≡ 1	day
7	days	≡ 1	week
1	year	≡	365 days
1	leap year	≡	366 days

For the months:

30 days hath September,
April, June, and November,
All the rest have 31,
Excepting February, which
Has 28 days clear,
But 29 in each leap year.

Time is based on the second, which is defined exactly. But a calendar needs to be based on a year, which is the period taken by the earth to go around the sun. This takes 365.2425 days, which, to give a workable system, means there must be a leap year every 4 years to adjust for that fraction of a day. That, by itself, gives a slight overcorrection, so every 100 years another correction is made. This leads to the rule that :

a leap year is a year whose number can be divided exactly by 4, except that when it is the beginning of a century it must be divided by 400. So 1996 and 2000 are leap years, but 1995 and 1900 were not.

Originally every system had its own standard on which the other measures were based. Now the SI (or metric) standards are accepted worldwide and all other measures are defined in terms of that. These values are exact:

1 yard ≡ 0.9144 meters	1 gallon (UK) ≡ 4.54609 liters
1 pound ≡ 0.453 592 37 kilograms	1 gallon (US liquid) ≡ 3.785 411 784 liters
	1 bushel (US dry) ≡ 35.239 070 166 88 liters

conversion factors are multipliers (or dividers) which can be used to change a numerical measure in one type of unit into its **equivalent measure** in another type of unit. The table below gives several conversion factors.

To change ...	*into* ...	multiply by ...	To change ...	*into* ...	multiply by ...
acres	*hectares*	0.4047	liters	*gallons (US)*	0.2642
acres	*sq miles*	0.001563	liters	*pints (UK)*	1.760
barrels (oil)	*gallons (UK)*	34.97	meters	*yards*	1.0936
barrels (oil)	*gallons (US)*	42*	miles	*kilometers*	1.609344*
centimeters	*inches*	0.3937	millimeters	*inches*	0.03937
cubic cm	*cu inches*	0.06102	ounces	*grams*	28.35
cubic feet	*cubic meters*	0.0283	pints (UK)	*liters*	0.5683
cubic feet	*gallons (UK)*	6.229	pints (US liquid)	*liters*	0.4732
cubic feet	*gallons (US)*	7.481	pounds	*kilograms*	0.4536
cubic inches	*cu cm*	16.39	square cm	*sq inches*	0.1550
cubic inches	*liters*	0.01639	square feet	*sq meters*	0.0929
cubic meters	*cubic feet*	35.31	square inches	*square cm*	6.4516*
feet	*meters*	0.3048*	square km	*square miles*	0.3861
gallons (UK)	*gallons (US)*	1.2009	square meters	*sq yards*	1.196
gallons (UK)	*liters*	4.54609*	square miles	*acres*	640*
gallons (US)	*gallons (UK)*	0.8327	square miles	*sq km*	2.590
gallons (US)	*liters*	3.785	square yards	*sq meters*	0.8361
grams	*ounces*	0.03527	tonnes	*kilograms*	1000*
hectares	*acres*	2.471	tonnes	*tons (long/UK)*	0.9842
hectares	*sq meters*	10000*	tonnes	*tons (short/US)*	1.1023
inches	*centimeters*	2.54*	tons (long/UK)	*kilograms*	1016
kilograms	*pounds*	2.2046	tons (long/UK)	*tonnes*	1.016
kilograms	*tons (long/UK)*	0.000984	tons (short/US)	*kilograms*	907.2
kilograms	*tons (short/US)*	0.001102	tons (short/US)	*tonnes*	0.9072
kilometers	*miles*	0.6214	yards	*meters*	0.9144*
liters	*cubic inches*	61.02			
liters	*gallons (UK)*	0.21997			

* indicates an **exact** figure; all others are approximations.

Some rough approximations for making comparisons (in the US) are:

1 kg	is about	2.2 lb	1 lb	is just under	0.5 kg
1 kg	is about	35 ounces	1 ounce	is just under	30 grams
1 km	is about	0.6 mile	1 mile	is about	1.6 km
1 meter	is just over	3 feet	1 foot	is about	30 cm
1 cm	is about	0.4 inch	1 inch	is about	2.5 cm
1 liter	is just over	0.25 gallon	1 gallon	is about	3.8 liters
1 liter	is about	2 pints	1 pint	is just under	0.5 liter

The International System of Units (usually identified as SI) officially came into being as the Système International d'Unités at the Eleventh General Conference of Weights and Measures, held in Paris in October 1960. There have been a few changes since then, such as the definition of a meter in 1983.

The SI defines seven base units. Four of these with their abbreviations (in parentheses) and definitions are:

meter (m) The meter is the unit of length. It is the distance light travels, in a vacuum, in $\frac{1}{299\,792\,458}$ th of a second.

kilogram (kg) The kilogram is the unit of mass. It is the mass of an international prototype in the form of a platinum-iridium cylinder kept at Sèvres in France. *It is now the only base unit still defined in terms of a material object, and also the only one with a prefix (kilo-) already in place.*

second (s) The second is the unit of time. It is the time taken for 9 192 631 770 periods of vibration of the caesium-133 atom to occur.

kelvin (K) The kelvin is the unit of thermodynamic temperature. It is $\frac{1}{273.16}$ th of the thermodynamic temperature of the triple point of water.
It is named after the Scottish mathematician and physicist William Thomson, First Lord Kelvin (1824–1907).

The other three base units are the ampere (A) for measuring current; the mole (mol) for measuring amounts of a substance; the candela (cd) for measuring the intensity of light.

There are two supplementary units: the **radian** for plane angular measure, and the steradian for "solid" or three-dimensional angles.

All other units are derived from these. For example, the unit of force is the newton which, in terms of the base units, is meter kilogram/second^2 or m kg s^{-2}

There are rules for using the SI. Some of the more important are:

- A unit may take only one **prefix**.
  Example: Millimillimeter is incorrect and should be micrometer.

- To make numbers easier to read, they may be divided into groups of three separated by spaces (or half-spaces) but NOT commas.

- Whole numbers should be separated from their decimal part by a comma. A point is acceptable but it must be placed on the line of the bottom edge of the number and not in a midway position.

convention for letters Many units are **eponyms**, named after a person closely associated with them (Newton, Watt, Pascal, etc). The convention for writing units which are eponyms is that when written in full their initial letter is in lower case, but their symbol or abbreviation is made with a capital letter. The one exception to this is the liter. It should be "l" (el) but, since that could be confused with "1" (one), the capital letter "L" is allowed. Some units and their abbreviations are:

becquerel	Bq	hertz	Hz	lux	lx
coulomb	C	joule	J	newton	N
farad	F	liter	l *or* L	pascal	Pa

prefixes A prefix is a group of letters placed at the beginning of a word to make a new word with a modified meaning. The SI allows other units to be created from the standard ones by using prefixes, which act as multipliers. This list gives the prefixes in most common use, the single letter or symbol to be used in the abbreviated form, and the multiplying factor they represent, both in **exponent** and in full. Note the difference between using capital letters and small letters.

exa-	**E**	$\times 10^{18}$	1 000 000 000 000 000 000
peta-	**P**	$\times 10^{15}$	1 000 000 000 000 000
tera-	**T**	$\times 10^{12}$	1 000 000 000 000
giga-	**G**	$\times 10^{9}$	1 000 000 000
mega-	**M**	$\times 10^{6}$	1 000 000
kilo-	**k**	$\times 10^{3}$	1 000
*hecto-	**h**	$\times 10^{2}$	100
*deca-	**da**	$\times 10^{1}$	10
		10^{0}	1
*deci-	**d**	$\times 10^{-1}$	0.1
*centi-	**c**	$\times 10^{-2}$	0.01
milli-	**m**	$\times 10^{-3}$	0.001
micro-	**μ**	$\times 10^{-6}$	0.000 001
nano-	**n**	$\times 10^{-9}$	0.000 000 001
pico-	**p**	$\times 10^{-12}$	0.000 000 000 001
femto-	**f**	$\times 10^{-15}$	0.000 000 000 000 001
atto-	**a**	$\times 10^{-18}$	0.000 000 000 000 000 001

*A prefix that is not actually in the SI but was in the original metric system and has remained in use because it has proved so convenient for everyday units.

Examples: *MW is megawatts or millions of watts.*
ns is nanoseconds or thousand-millionths of a second.

Some standard values given in SI units are:

nautical mile The international nautical mile is 1852 meters.

knot A knot is a speed of 1 nautical mile per hour.

gravitational acceleration The rate of acceleration on the earth's surface as a result of gravity is 9.806 65 meters per second squared.

speed of light The speed of light is 2.9979×10^{8} meters per second.

light year A light year is a distance of 9.4605×10^{15} meters.

earth's radius The mean radius of the earth is 6.371×10^{6} meters.

earth's mass The mass of the earth is 5.977×10^{24} kilograms.

earth-to-moon distance The mean distance is 3.844×10^{8} meters.

earth-to-sun distance The mean distance is 1.496×10^{11} meters.

vector A vector is something which can be defined by two quantities: its size and its direction.
Examples: Velocity is a vector, since it is described by giving both the speed of an object and the direction in which the object is moving. Speed alone is not a vector. Force is also a vector.

AB and $\overrightarrow{AB}$ are two of the symbols used in diagrammatic and written work to refer to a **vector** whose size is represented by the distance between A and B and whose direction is from A to B. *The size is often referred to some scale. A single letter is also used (A or a or A etc.) but only after the vector has been defined in some way.*

scalar A scalar is a quantity which can be completely defined by a single number. *It may or it may not have units attached.*
Examples: Length, mass, speed, and numbers are all scalar quantities.

plane vector A plane vector is a **vector** whose direction can be given solely by reference to two-dimensional space. *This might be done by using coordinates such as (x,y), or by using an angle such as a compass direction.*

position vector A position vector is a **vector** which starts at some known point, and its finishing point gives a position relative to that starting point. *Any coordinate system may be thought of as a vector system, where the origin is the starting point of a position vector which then goes to (or finishes at) the given position.*

free vector A free vector is a **vector** which does not have a defined starting point and so can be placed anywhere in space.
Example: Any translation can be defined by a single free vector.

absolute value The absolute value of a **vector** is its size. *Direction is ignored.*

scalar multiplication Scalar multiplication of a **vector** is carried out by multiplying the size of a vector by a single number. *Direction is unchanged.*

unit vector A unit vector is a **vector** which is to be considered as being the unit of size from which other vectors are made by **scalar multiplication**.

negative vector The negative of a given **vector** is another vector that is the same in size but opposite in direction to the given vector.

orthogonal vectors are **vectors** whose directions are at right angles to each other.

vector addition Two or more **vectors** can be added by joining them together end to end, always so that their directions "follow on" from each other, and the answer is the single vector which can be drawn from the "start" point to the "finish" point of the vectors. *The order in which they are joined does not matter. Subtraction is done by the addition of a negative vector.*

resultant A resultant is the **vector** produced by the addition and/or subtraction of two or more vectors. *It is the single vector which can replace all the other vectors and still produce the same result.*

vector triangle A vector triangle is made when three **vectors** are added together to form a triangle whose **resultant** is zero.

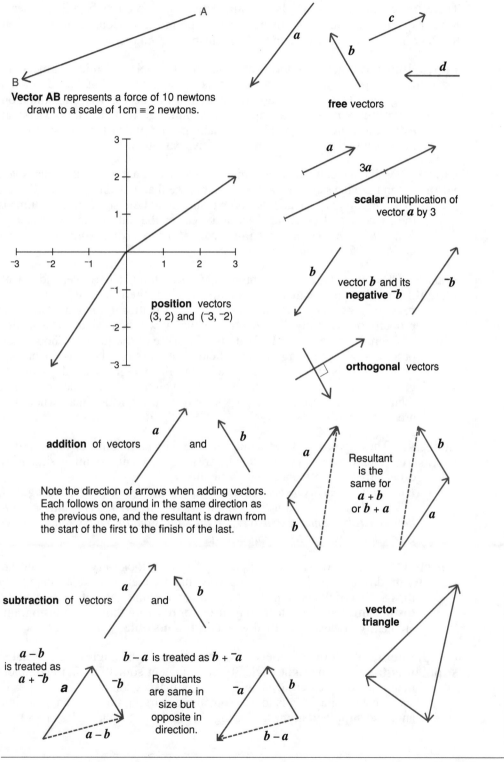

Vector AB represents a force of 10 newtons drawn to a scale of 1cm ≡ 2 newtons.

free vectors

position vectors
(3, 2) and (⁻3, ⁻2)

scalar multiplication of vector **a** by 3

vector **b** and its **negative** ⁻**b**

orthogonal vectors

addition of vectors **a** and **b**

Note the direction of arrows when adding vectors. Each follows on around in the same direction as the previous one, and the resultant is drawn from the start of the first to the finish of the last.

a

b

Resultant is the same for **a** + **b** or **b** + **a**

b

a

subtraction of vectors **a** and **b**

vector triangle

a − **b** is treated as **a** + ⁻**b**

a

⁻**b**

a − **b**

b − **a** is treated as **b** + ⁻**a**

Resultants are same in size but opposite in direction.

⁻**a**

b

b − **a**

word confusions

There are several pairs of words in mathematics which seem to be alike, either in look or in meaning. Some are given in their appropriate section, but some are put together in this section with help to distinguish between them.

approximation These two terms are often used as being identical in meaning,
estimation because an estimation is an approximation based upon a judgment. However, an approximation is not necessarily an estimation. An **approximation** is applied to a number that already exists; an **estimation** creates a number by making a judgment that is usually (but not always) derived from an actual physical situation.

capacity Mathematically these both measure the size of a three-dimensional space
volume and use the same units. It is in their usage that they differ: capacity refers to a containing space and the room available to hold something; volume is the space actually occupied by an object or the bulk of some substance. *Example: A bucket has a **capacity** of 20 liters so the **volume** of water needed to fill the bucket is 20 liters.*

mass These two words are commonly used as though they were identical.
weight This does not matter for ordinary use, but there is a difference. The **mass** of a body is a measure of how much matter it contains and is the property of that body that governs the way it will behave under the action of a force. The **weight** of a body is a measure of the force the body itself produces when in a gravitational field. The mass of a body is unchanged wherever it is in the universe, whereas the weight depends upon the gravitational force at the place it is being weighed. Objects do not change their mass, but certainly weigh less, when on the Moon than when they are on the earth.

inclusive These words, used to indicate whether something is to be put in
exclusive (included) or not (excluded), are often used in counting situations, especially with reference to the calendar.
Examples: "The insurance coverage runs from August 5, 1997 to August 4, 1998 inclusive," so both the given dates are covered. "The sale will run between July 3 and 9 exclusive," so the sale is on for 5 days, since the two given dates are not to be counted in.

bar chart These two types of frequency diagrams look very similar and are
histogram differentiated only by the way the frequency is represented: by the LENGTH of the bars in the **bar chart** and by the AREA of the bars in the **histogram**. Bar charts tend to be used for **discrete data** while histograms are nearly always concerned with **continuous data**.

complementary Both of these, when referred to angles, are related
supplementary to the right angle. To complement something is to complete it, and so **complementary** angles together make a complete right angle. To supplement something is to add something extra, in this case another right angle, so **supplementary** angles together make two right angles or 180°

congruent These two words are used to compare geometrical shapes.
similar **Congruent** is much stronger, since the two shapes being compared must be identical to each other in every way, except that one may be turned around, or over, in relation to the other. **Similar** requires only that the two shapes be identical in their shape, and one may be bigger than the other. *Example: Given one large and one small square, they are similar but not congruent.*

conjecture The difference between these two words is mainly one of usage.
hypothesis Both are unproved statements for which, usually, a lot of supporting evidence can be found. **Conjectures** are generally about numbers and allow NO exceptions. **Hypotheses** generally occur in statistics, are usually set up before a search is carried out for supporting evidence, often involve a probability as to their correctness, and are sometimes put in a negative form to make it easier to search for evidence that they are wrong.

possible An event is described as possible if it is within the bounds of reason
probable that it could happen; otherwise it is impossible. It is described as probable if the chance of it happening is a good one. Though "good" is not defined, common usage implies that a probable event is one that is more likely to happen than not. *Example: Someone could say about a racehorse that is not very good: "It is possible for this horse to win, but not probable."*

necessary Consider two related statements P and Q, ordered P first and Q
sufficient second. If, whenever P is true then Q must also be true, then P is a **sufficient** condition for Q. If, whenever P is false then Q must also be false, then P is a **necessary** condition for Q. *Example: Referring to a quadrilateral, the following statements are made:*

Q *is "It is a parallelogram."*
P′ *is "Two opposite sides are equal in length."*
P″ *is "All its sides are equal in length."*
P‴ *is "Two opposite sides are parallel and equal in length."*
Then, in relation to statement Q*:*

P′ *is necessary;*   P″ *is sufficient;*   P‴ *is necessary and sufficient*

partition Both of these words describe a type of division applied to a
quotition physical situation, where whatever is being divided is named, or has units attached. If the **dividend** and **divisor** have DIFFERENT types of names it is a partition; if they have the SAME type of name it is a quotition. *Examples: Dividing (sharing) 100 apples among 10 people is a partition (apples ÷ people). Finding how many 10 cm lengths can be cut from a 1-meter strip is a quotition (length ÷ length).*

disc There is no difference in the meanings of these, only in the spelling.
disk Currently there is a difference in usage, with dis**k** being used for a computer disk and dis**c** for a compact disc. *The k usage will probably win.*

Many of the words used in English (especially those in mathematics) were originally taken from, or based upon, the ancient languages of Greek and Latin. Some of these connections can be seen from this table.

Meaning	Greek	Latin	Used in
something learned	mathema		mathematics
small stone		calculus	calculate, calculus
to be worth		valere	value, evaluate
number	arithmos	numerus	arithmetic
one	hen	unus	unit
two	di	bi	diagonal, bisect
three	treis	tres	triangle, trisect
four	tetra	quadri	tetrahedron, quadrilateral
five	pente	quinque	pentagon, quintic
six	hexe	sex	hexagon, sextant
seven	hepta	septem	heptagon, September
eight	okta	octo	octagon, October
nine	ennea	nonus	enneagon, nonagon
ten	deka	decem	decagon, December
twelve	dodeka	duodecem	dodecagon, duodecimal
hundred	hekaton	centum	hectare, percent
thousand	khilioi	mille	kilogram, per mil
many	polion	polium	polygon, polyhedron
one-tenth		decimus	decimal
first	protos	primo	prototype, prime
single	monos	singularus	monopoly, singular
double		duplicatus	duplicate
half	hemi	semi	hemisphere, semicircle
corner	gonos	angulus	hexagon, angle
small circus	kirkos	circulus	circle
measure across	diametros	diametrus	diameter
round		circum	circumference
string	khorde	chorda	chord
to cut	secare		segment, secant
wheel		rota	rotate
roller	kulindros	cylindrus	cylinder
coil	speira	spira	spiral
done with care		accuratus	accurate
go astray		errare	error
land measuring	geometria		geometry
equal legs	isoskeles		isosceles triangle
unequal	skalenos		scalene triangle

Meaning	Greek	Latin	Used in
lying near		adjacere	adjacent
sharp		acutus	acute angle
blunt		obtusus	obtuse angle
maker		factor	factor
crowd		frequentia	frequency
thing given		datum	data
middle		medius	median
breaking		fractio	fraction
to name		denominare	denominator
to touch		tangere	tangent
heart-shaped	kardioeides		cardioid
kidney	nephros		nephroid
ball or globe	sphaira		sphere
sawn across	prisma		prism
separate	horizein		horizon
follow		sequi	sequence
join together		serere	series
foundation	hupothesis		hypothesis
put together		conjicere	conjecture
speculation	theorema		theorem
mark or token	sumbolon		symbol
a step		gradus	gradient
dwarf	nanos	nanus	nanosecond
great	megas		megahertz
giant	gigas		gigahertz

Plurals

A result of using words from other languages is in the way plurals can be formed. Many are now seen with the *-s* or *-es* ending of standard English, but the following list gives the singular and plural forms of some words in mathematics which can take a different ending.

abscissa	abscissae	frustum	frusta	minimum	minima
apex	apices	helix	helices	parabola	parabolae
axis	axes	hyperbola	hyperbolae	polygon	polygona
datum	data*	hypothesis	hypotheses	polyhedron	polyhedra
die	dice	index	indices	radius	radii
directrix	directrices	locus	loci	rhombus	rhombi
focus	foci	matrix	matrices	trapezium	trapezia
formula	formulae	maximum	maxima	vertex	vertices

*Data, when used in statistics and computing, is increasingly used only as a singular collective noun – *"the data is"* rather than *"the data are."*

curve In most cases curve is used to describe a line that is not straight. However, general use in mathematics requires that straight lines be included.
Example: "Join the points with a curve" allows a straight line to be drawn if that is appropriate.

clockwise The direction of a movement around a circular arc is described as being clockwise if it moves in the same direction, relative to the center, as that of the hands of a conventional clock.

counterclockwise A counterclockwise direction is one which is opposite to **clockwise**.

certain An event can be described as certain only if it MUST happen.

likely In ordinary use, an event is described as being likely if it has a better chance of happening than NOT happening. In mathematics, likely is more often used as having the same meaning as **probable**.
Examples: *"It is likely I shall go to town tomorrow."*
"How likely is it that I shall throw a 4 with this die?"

circumscribe A second shape is said to circumscribe a first shape if the second completely the encloses the first, touching it at several points but not cutting it. *It is usual to require the circumscribing shape to be the smallest possible under the conditions given. The most common examples are the circumcircle to a polygon and the circumsphere to a polyhedron. The drawing on the right shows a regular hexagon circumscribing an irregular quadrilateral.*

inscribe A second shape is said to be inscribed in a first shape if the second is completely inside the first, touching it at several points but not cutting it. *It is usual to require the inscribed shape to be the largest possible under the conditions given. The most common examples are the incircle to a polygon and the in-sphere to a polyhedron. The drawing above shows an irregular quadrilateral inscribed in a regular hexagon.*

difference In ordinary use, the difference between two things requires a description of the ways in which they are not alike, but, in arithmetic, a difference is the result of subtracting one number from another.
Example: The difference between 4 and 6 could be described as being "one is all straight lines while the other is curved," but arithmetically it is 2

bisect To bisect an object, usually a line or a shape, is to cut, or divide, it into two parts which are equal in size and shape.

prefix A prefix is the first part of a word that controls the meaning of the whole word. *The most commonly used prefixes are: bi- (= 2); tri- (= 3); quad- or tetra- (= 4); pent- or quinque- (= 5); hex- or sex- (= 6); hept- or sept- (=7); oct- (=8).*
Examples: Triangle is made from the prefix tri- (= 3) + angle. Pentagon is pent- (=5) + gon (which comes from the Greek for angle).
SI units also make use of prefixes to make bigger or smaller units.

magnitude The magnitude of something is a measure of its size.